Leading Schools Legally, IN Supplement: The ABC's of School Law

Written by:
Jeffery Qualkinbush
Bruce Donaldson

Contributing Editors:
David Emmert, Esq.
Dr. William Roberson
Dr. Charles Hobbs
Dr. Al Long
Dr. Brad Balch

ISBN 0-9748391-7-5

Power Publishing
5641 West 73rd Street
Indianapolis, IN 46278
(317) 347-1051

Copyright © 2006 by Power Publishing

All rights reserved. No part of this book may be reproduced without written permission from the publisher, except by a reviewer who may quote brief passages in a review; nor may any part of this book be reproduced, stored in a retrieval system or transmitted in any form or other without written permission from the publisher.

This book is manufactured in the United States of America.

Library of Congress Cataloging in Publication Data in Progress.

Published by Power Publishing
5641 West 73rd Street
Indianapolis, IN 46278

Special thanks to Barnes & Thornburg LLP for providing the funding for the Leading Schools Legally project.

Contents at a Glance

Article I: Building Projects, Borrowing, Budgeting & Bargaining

Part I: Building

Public Contsruction	9
Common Construction Wage Process	19
Guaranteed Energy Savings Contracts	23
Acquisition & Disposition of Equipment	27

Part II: Borrowing

General Obligation Bonds	43
Lease Finanacing	49
Miscellaneous Financing Methods	59
Petition-Remonstrance Process	67

Part III: Budgeting

Budgets, Appropriations and Public Fund Laws	75
The Primary Funds of a School Corporation	83
General Fund Referendum Process	91

Part IV: Bargaining

Collective Bargaining	97
Unfair Practices	107

Article II: The ABC's of School Law

The ABC's of School Law
See Section for Detailed Table of Contents	113

INTRODUCTION

This supplement is designed with a two-fold goal in mind. First, as a guide for funding of building projects as well as school finance issues, including collective bargaining. The second portion is designed as a quick reference document to aid in the everyday leading of a school and/or a school corporation.

This document is also designed to be a supplement to the book "Leading Schools Legally". In many areas, the supplement will make references for the reader to go to the main book for specific cases and more detailed information.

Nothing in this document should be construed as legal advice or opinion. The school or school corporation should consult their local counsel or bond counsel if a question arises. This is a guide for administrators, boards and future administrators to use when contemplating a legal issue.

ARTICLE I

BUILDING PROJECTS, BORROWING, BUDGETING, & BARGAINING

PART I

BUILDING

PUBLIC CONSTRUCTION

I. GENERAL

A. Applicability

Any construction, reconstruction, alteration or renovation of a school building, facility or other structure, which is paid from any fund held by the school corporation or from the proceeds of any financing which is repaid, in whole or in part, from funds of the school corporation, must comply with the Indiana public construction laws. These laws also apply to any publicly funded project regardless of whether the work is performed on property owned or leased by the school corporation.

B. Exceptions

1. A project which qualifies as a guaranteed energy savings project under Indiana Code 36-1-12.5, as amended, is not subject to the requirements of the Indiana public construction laws except for the common construction wage laws and anti-discriminatory laws. (Refer to "Guaranteed Energy Savings Contracts" later in Part I.)

2. The Indiana public construction laws do not apply to the awarding and entering into of contracts for the professional services of (a) architects, (b) engineers, (c) construction managers, (d) surveyors, (e) appraisers, (f) attorneys, (g) financial advisors, and (h) underwriters. However, a school board may not employ the architect or engineer who provided design services on a public construction project or his affiliate, to be the construction manager on the project designed by the architect. In addition, a school board may not award to the construction manager of the project a general contract or any separate trade contract to perform work on that project. Finally, no professional other than an underwriter or a real estate broker may be paid a fee which is based on a percentage of the project cost.

3. A school corporation is not required to comply with the Indiana public construction laws in connection with any construction project if (a) the school corporation uses its own workforce for that project, (b) the estimated cost of the entire project, including the cost of materials, labor, equipment, rental, a reasonable rate for use of school corporation trucks and heavy equipment, and all other expenses incidental to the performance of the project, is less than $100,000, and (c) the school corporation has a group of employees on its staff who are capable of performing the construction, maintenance, and repair work required by the project.

C. Violation of the Indiana Public Construction Laws

1. Any contract for a public work project, which is not let in accordance with the Indiana public construction laws, is void.

2. A school corporation may not divide the cost of a single project into two or more projects for the purpose of avoiding the requirements under the Indiana public construction laws. For the purposes of the Indiana public construction laws, the cost of the public work project includes the cost of materials, labor, equipment rental and all other expenses incidental to the performance of the project. Any bidder or submitter of the quote who is a party to a public work contract, who knowingly violates this law, commits a Class A infraction and may be precluded from being a party to any contract under the Indiana public construction laws for two years from the date of the conviction. Any school board member or officer of the school corporation, who knowingly violates this law, commits a Class A infraction.

II. PUBLIC WORKS PROJECTS COSTING LESS THAN $25,000

A. General

If a public works project is estimated to cost less than $25,000, the school board may comply with the procedures for public works projects estimated to cost $25,000 or more. (Refer to "Public Works Projects Costing $25,000 or More" in Section III, of this Part I.) Alternatively, for public works projects which are estimated to cost less than $25,000, the school board may proceed with a simpler invitation process.

B. Procedural Steps and Other Requirements

1. A school board electing to award a contract by invitation to quote must:

    (a) invite quotes from at least three people or companies known to deal in the class of work proposed to be done by mailing them a notice stating that plans and specifications are on file in a specified office; the notice must be mailed not less than seven days before the time fixed for receiving quotes;

    (b) not require a person to submit a quote before the meeting at which quotes are to be received;

    (c) receive all quotes at a meeting which is open to the public, at which time all quotes which are received must be opened in public and read aloud; and

    (d) award the contract for the public work to the lowest responsible and responsive person or company providing a quote.

2. The school board may reject all quotes submitted. If the school board rejects all quotes, then it may negotiate and enter into agreements for the work in the open market without inviting or receiving quotes if the school board establishes in writing the reasons for rejecting the quotes.

3. All plans and specifications prepared for such projects must be approved by

PUBLIC CONSTRUCTION 11

the State Department of Health, the State Fire Marshal and the State Building Commissioner.

4. Any person or entity submitting a quote for a public works project that involves the installation of plumbing must submit evidence that the person or entity is licensed plumbing contractor under Indiana Code 25-28.5-1, as amended.

5. If steel products are anticipated to be used in the public works project, the specifications must require that all such steel products must be manufactured in the United States unless the cost is unreasonable.

III. PUBLIC WORKS PROJECTS COSTING $25,000 OR MORE

A. General

If a public works project is estimated to cost $25,000 or more, the school corporation must comply with the public bidding requirements set forth in this section.

B. Procedural Steps

1. Specifications and Bidding Requirements

    (a) General. The school board must prepare general plans and specifications describing the kind of public works required but should avoid specifications which might unduly limit competition. All plans and specifications must be approved by the State Department of Health, the State Fire Marshal and the State Building Commissioner. The school board must file the plans and specifications in a place reasonably accessible to the public, which must be specified in the notice to bidders. The school board must require each bidder to submit an affidavit that (a) the bidder has not entered into a combination or agreement (i) relative to the price bid by another bidder; (ii) to prevent a person or entity from bidding; or (iii) to induce a person or entity to refrain from bidding and (b) the bidder's bid is made without reference to any other bid. In addition, the school board may not require the bidder to submit a bid before the meeting at which bids are to be received.

    (b) Plumbing Projects. Any person or entity submitting a bid for a public works project that involves the installation of plumbing must submit evidence that the person or entity is licensed plumbing contractor under Indiana Code 25-28.5-1, as amended.

    (c) Steel Products. If steel products are anticipated to be used in the public works project, the specifications must require that all such steel products must be manufactured in the United States unless the cost is unreasonable.

    (d) Projects costing more than $100,000. If the cost of the project is $100,000 or more, the plans and specifications must be approved by an architect or engineer, who is licensed pursuant to Indiana Code 25-4 or Indiana Code 25-31. In addition, if the cost of the project is $100,000 or more the school board must require each bidder to submit a financial statement, a statement of experience, its proposed plan or plans for performing the public work, and the equipment that it has available for the performance of the public work. This statement must be submitted on forms prescribed by the State Board of Accounts. Finally, within sixty (60) days of completion of the project, the school corporation must file with the State Building Commissioner a complete set of final record drawings for the public work project. The State Building Commissioner must provide a depository for all final record drawings filed and retain them for inspection, use or storage as provided by Indiana Code § 36-1-12-11.

2.   Notice of Receipt of Bids

Upon approving the final plans and specifications for the project, the school board must publish a notice which requests sealed proposals for the public work, which specifies the place where the plans and specifications are on file and the date for receiving bids. This notice must also include (a) a statement that a bond or certified check, which is made payable to the school corporation, is required to be filed with each bid by the bidder, and (b) the amount of each such bond or certified check. The amount of each such bond or certified may not be more than ten percent of the bid. This notice must be published twice in one or two local newspapers, published or generally circulated in the school corporation, with at least one week between the first and second publication in the same newspaper. In addition, the second publication must be at least one week prior to the date on which sealed proposals are to be submitted.

3.   Receiving and Awarding of Bid

(a)   The meeting for receiving bids must be open to the public. All bids received must be opened publicly and read aloud at the time and place designated in the notice to bidders. The school board may (a) award the bid to the lowest responsible and responsive bidder or (b) reject all bids as submitted. If the bid and contract are awarded to a bidder other than the lowest bidder, the school board must state in the minutes or memoranda of the meeting at the time the award is made the factors used to justify the award. The minutes or memoranda must be retained by the school corporation and be made available for public inspection.

(b)   In determining whether a bidder is responsive, the school board may consider the following factors:

(i)   whether the bidder has submitted a bid or quote that conforms in

PUBLIC CONSTRUCTION

all material respects to the specifications;

(ii) whether the bidder has submitted a bid that complies specifically with the invitation to bid and the instructions to bidders; and

(iii) whether the bidder has complied with all applicable statutes, ordinances, resolutions, or rules pertaining to the award of a public contract.

(c) In determining whether a bidder is a responsible bidder, the school board may consider the following factors:

(i) the ability and capacity of the bidder to perform the work;

(ii) the integrity, character, and reputation of the bidder; and

(iii) the competence and experience of the bidder.

(d) The school board must award the contract and issue the written notice to proceed with the project within sixty days after the date on which bids are opened unless:

(i) general obligation bonds are sold to finance the project in which case the school board must award the contract and issue the written notice to proceed with the project within ninety days after the date on which bids are opened; or

(ii) revenue bonds are sold to finance the project in which case the school board must award the contract and issue the written notice to proceed with the project within one hundred fifty days after the date on which bids are opened.

(e) If the school board fails to award and execute the contract and issue the notice to proceed with the project within the timeframes set forth in the immediately preceding paragraph, the successful bidder may:

(i) reject the contract and withdraw the successful bid without prejudice; or

(ii) extend the time to award the contract and provide notice to proceed at an agreed later date. If the successful bidder chooses to withdraw the bid and reject the contract, notice of the election must be given by the successful bidder to the school corporation in writing within fifteen days of the expiration of the timeframes set forth in the immediately preceding paragraph.

(f)   All checks of unsuccessful bidders must be returned upon selection of the successful bidder. Checks of successful bidders should be held until delivery of the performance bond.

IV. CONTRACTS UPON DECLARATION OF EMERGENCY

The school board, upon a declaration of emergency, may contract for a public work project without advertising for bids if bids or quotes are invited from at least two people or entities known to perform the type of public work required to be done. The minutes of the school board must show the declaration of emergency and the names of the people or companies invited to bid or provide quotes.

V. CONTRACT ISSUES WITH CONTRACTORS

A. Required Terms in all Contracts

1.   Each contract for a public work must contain a provision for the payment of subcontractors, laborers, material suppliers, and those performing services. The school board will withhold money from the contract price in a sufficient amount to pay the subcontractors, laborers, material suppliers, and other entities furnishing services.

2.   If one or more subcontractors, material suppliers, laborers, or other entities furnishing services in connection with the project file a claim for payment with the school corporation within sixty days after the last labor is performed, last material furnished or last service rendered by them, the school board must withhold the final payment to the contractor until the contractor has paid the subcontractors, material suppliers, laborers, or other entities furnishing services or may pay all such claims from the final payment due to the contractor and deduct it from the final payment owed to the contractor by the school corporation. If the final payment to the contractor is less than the amounts owed by the contractor to the subcontractors, material suppliers, laborers, or those furnishing services, the school corporation will pay to each subcontractor, material supplier, laborer, or entity furnishing services a prorated amount of that final payment. If there is a dispute between the contractor and the claiming party or parties, the school board will retain sufficient money to pay the claims until the dispute is settled and the correct amount is determined.

3.   A school corporation must pay interest on amounts due on public works contracts if such amounts are not paid at the time specified in the contract document or thirty-five (35) days after the receipt of a properly completed claim. The amount of interest to be paid is equal to 1% of the amount due for each month until paid. Any contractor receiving late payment penalties from the school corporation must make interest payments to the subcontractor at the same rate of interest.

4.   All public works projects must conform with the common construction wage laws of Indiana Code 5-16-7, as amended. (Refer to "Common Construction Wage Process" later in this Part I.)

PUBLIC CONSTRUCTION

5. All public works project must conform with the antidiscrimination provisions of Indiana Code 5-16-6, as amended. The school corporation may consider failure by the contractor to comply with these provisions as a material breach of the public works contract.

B. Required Terms in Contracts in Excess of $100,000

1. Retainage.

   (a) All contracts between the school corporation or affiliated entity and the contractors must include contract provisions for the retainage of portions of the payments to the contractors. If a contractor subcontracts all or any portion of the contractor's work, the contract between the contractor and the subcontractor must also include contract provisions for the retainage of portions of the payments to the subcontractors. The school corporation is not required to pay interest on the amounts of retainage it holds under the contracts but it is required to pay any interest on retainage held by an escrow agent.

   (b) At the discretion of the contractor, the retainage may be held by the school corporation or placed in an escrow account with a bank, savings and loan institution or the state as the escrow agent as determined by the parties to the contract or the subcontract. If the retainage is held by an escrow agent a written agreement must be executed to establish such retainage account. The escrow agreement must require (i) the escrow agent to invest all escrowed principal in obligations selected by the escrow agent, (ii) the escrow agent to hold the escrowed principal and income until receipt of notice from the school board and the contractor, or the contractor and the subcontractor, as the case may be, specifying the part of the escrowed principal to be released from the escrow and the person to whom that portion is to be released, and (iii) payment of the fees of the escrow agent from the escrowed income.

   (c) Under Indiana law, the school board has two retainage options. One option is to retain 10% of the contract payments due for all work which is satisfactorily completed until the public work is 50% completed, at which time no more retainage is held. The other option is to retain 5% of the contract payments due for all work which is satisfactorily completed until the public work is substantially completed.

   (d) Within 61 days after substantial completion of the project, the school corporation or the escrow agent, if any, must pay the contractor the retainage for all work which is completed. If within 61 days after substantial completion there remains uncompleted minor items, the school corporation or escrow agent will retain an amount equal to 200% of the estimated value of the uncompleted work until such items are completed.

PART I: BUILDING PROJECTS

2. Payment Bond

    (a) The contractor must execute and deliver a payment bond to the school corporation in form to be approved by and for the benefit of the school corporation in an amount equal to the contract price. The payment bond must also state it is for the benefit of the subcontractors, laborers, material suppliers and other entities performing services in connection with the project. Under the terms of the standard payment bond, the surety of the payment bond agrees to pay the material suppliers, subcontractors, laborers and other entities furnishing services for material provided or work performed by such entities in the event they are not paid by the contractor. Therefore, the payment bond protects the school corporation from any liens being placed on the school corporation's property and reduces the likelihood of any claim for payment being filed against the school corporation by a material supplier, a subcontractor or other worker.

    (b) The payment bond must be deposited with the school board and must specify that the payment bond remains in full force and effect regardless of (i) any modification, omission or addition to the terms and conditions of the public work, plans, specifications, drawings, or profile, (ii) any defect in the contract, or (iii) any defect in the proceedings preliminary to the letting and awarding of the contract. The surety of the payment bond may not be released until one year after the school board's final settlement with the contractor.

3. Performance Bond

    (a) The contractor must provide the school corporation with a performance bond in an amount equal to the contract price for the benefit of the school corporation. Under the terms of the standard performance bond, the surety of the performance bond agrees to pay the school corporation an amount up to the contract price to compensate the school corporation for any damage it suffers as a result of the contractor's failure to perform the contractor's obligations under the contract, including any warranty obligations. The performance bond must specify that it remains in full force and effect regardless of (i) any modification, omission or addition to the terms and conditions of the public work, plans, specifications, drawings, or profile, (ii) any defect in the contract, or (iii) any defect in the proceedings preliminary to the letting and awarding of the contract. The performance bond may provide for incremental bonding in the form of multiple or chronological bonds, that, when taken as a whole, equal the contract price. The surety may not be released until one (1) year after the date of the political subdivision's final settlement with the contractor.

PUBLIC CONSTRUCTION

(b)   The school board may waive the performance bond on contracts for projects which are estimated to cost less than $250,000 and accept from a contractor an irrevocable letter of credit for an equivalent amount from an Indiana financial institution approved by the State Department of Financial Institutions.

C. Change Orders

Change orders for the addition, deletion or change of an item may be issued as an addendum to the contract when approved by the school board and contractor. When a licensed architect or engineer is assigned to the project the change order must be prepared by the architect or engineer. A change order must (a) not be issued prior to commencement of the actual work, except in cases of emergency, (b) not increase the scope of the project in an aggregate amount greater than 20% of the original contract amount, and (c) be directly related to the original public work project. A change order issued as a result of circumstances that could not be reasonably foreseen is deemed to not increase the scope of the project. The cost of any additional material supplies must be at the same unit cost as identified in the original contract.

VI.   PROJECTS IN EXCESS OF $1,000,000

If a school corporation anticipates spending more than $1,000,000 in connection with a construction, renovation or expansion project, it must hold a public hearing on the project. This public hearing is commonly called the "1028 Public Hearing" because it was enacted by Public Law 1028. This public hearing is required regardless of the source of repayment of the project. Notice for this hearing must be published only one time in one or two newspapers published or generally circulated in the boundaries of the school corporation. The notice must be published at least ten days prior to the public hearing. At the public hearing, the school corporation should receive information regarding the general educational purpose of the project, the proposed site for the building, the estimated cost of the project, the estimated completion date of the project, the funding sources for the project, the estimated impact of the project on the school corporation's tax rate, the year in which that tax rate impact is anticipated to occur and any other relevant information. Following the presentation of this information, the school board must provide all members of the community the opportunity to provide comments regarding the project and the information presented. Subsequent to such public comment, the school board must adopt a resolution approving the general educational purpose of the project, the proposed site for the building, the estimated cost of the project, the estimated completion date of the project, the funding sources for the project, the estimated impact of the project on the school corporation's tax rate, the year in which that tax rate impact is anticipated to occur and any other relevant information.

COMMON CONSTRUCTION WAGE PROCESS

I. GENERAL

A. Requirement

Indiana's common construction wage statute requires any firm, individual, partnership, limited liability company, or corporation that is awarded a contract by the school corporation for the construction of a public work, and any subcontractor of the construction, to pay for each class of work at a scale of wages which is not less than the common construction wage, as such terms are defined by Indiana law. A public work includes any public project which is paid for out of public funds, including any public project that will be: (i) owned entirely; or (ii) leased with an option to purchase, by the school corporation. The common construction wage means a scale of wages for each class of work that is not less than the common construction wage of all construction wages being paid in the county where the project is located, as determined by the common construction wage committee.

B. Exceptions

The two types of school corporation projects which are exempt from the common construction wage laws are (1) public projects which are to be paid for in whole or in part with funds granted by the federal government, unless the department of the federal government making the grant consents in writing to the application of the common construction wage laws, and (2) public projects in which the actual construction costs will be less than $150,000.

II. WAGE DETERMINATION PROCESS

A. Establishing a Wage Committee

Prior to advertising for the contract, the school board must establish a committee of five people, which will determine the common construction wage in the county where the project is located. The school board makes two appointments to the committee. One of those school board appointments must be a taxpayer who is paying taxes which will serve as the funding source for the project. This person is often a member of the school board. The other school board appointment does not have to be a taxpayer in the community, but must be a representative of the construction industry. This person is often the architect or the construction manager. After these two people are appointed, the school corporation's attorney or representative contacts the county legislative body and requests an appointment to the committee by them. This person must be a taxpayer who is paying taxes which will serve as the funding source for the project. Depending on the county in which the project is located, the county legislative body will differ. Therefore, you need to have this determination made by the school corporation's attorney and bond counsel.

After this person is appointed, the school corporation's attorney or representative provides written notice to the Wage and Hour Division of the Indiana Department of Labor that a common construction wage committee has been established by the school corporation for a specific set of projects. In this written notice, the school corporation requests the appointment of the final two members to the committee and the establishment of a date, time and place for the common construction wage committee. The final two members of the committee are an appointment from the Indiana Governor and an appointment by the state federation of labor (the AFL-CIO). The appointment by the AFL-CIO represents labor. After these appointments are made, the school corporation will receive a copy of the letter sent by the Wage and Hour Division of the Indiana Department of Labor to each member of the common construction wage committee identifying the date, time and location of the meeting of the committee, which will be in the county where the project is located. As soon as the school corporation receives that letter, the school corporation or its attorney should contact all three local members of the committee to make sure they received the letter and they will be able to attend the meeting. By making this contact early, the school corporation helps to ensure a quorum will be present at the meeting. The meeting of this committee is required to comply with the Indiana Open Door Law, and those matters will be handled by the State Department of Labor.

B. Responsibilities of the Committee

The committee is responsible for (1) determining which trades or crafts will be employed at the project and (2) the minimum wages to be paid by all contractors and subcontractors which will work on the project. These determinations must be made at least two weeks prior to the school corporation or its representative publish a notice advertising for receipt of bids for the project. The minimum wages must be divided into skilled labor, semiskilled labor and unskilled labor for each trade or craft, and cannot be less than the common construction wage for each of the three classes of labor currently being paid in the county where the project is located. In making these determinations, the committee must consider any reports from the Indiana Department of Labor and any other information submitted by any person to the committee. The Indiana Court of Appeals has clearly stated in *Union Township School Corp. v. State ex rel. Joyce*, 706 N.E.2d 183 (Ind. Ct. App. 1998) the committee must determine the wages that are most commonly/frequently paid in the community according to the labor classifications, and the committee may not select an average when making its determination. In addition, the Indiana Court of Appeals determined in the Union Township case that the term wage includes fringe benefits. If the committee fails to make or file a determination on the wage scale at least two weeks prior to the date fixed for the advertising of construction bids, the school board must make the common construction wage determination, and its finding will be final. If the project is being financed through the issuance of bonds or a lease payable from a school corporation's debt service fund, the school corporation must file this wage determination with the School Property Tax Control Board as a part of its hearing information sheet for the financing.

III. COMPLIANCE WITH THE COMMON CONSTRUCTION WAGE STATUTE

A. Compliance Requirements

Under Indiana law, a school corporation must require as a condition to bidding on any public construction project, the bidder agree, that if the bidder is awarded the contract, the bidder and all subcontractors will strictly comply with the wage determination made by the common construction wage committee. In addition, the school corporation must require all contractors or subcontractors performing work on the project to file a schedule of the wages to be paid to laborers, workmen, or mechanics prior to performing any work on the project.

B. Penalties for Violation

A contractor or subcontractor who knowingly fails to pay the rate of wages determined by the common construction wage committee commits a Class B misdemeanor. If the contractor or subcontractor has committed a prior offense, the contract on which the instant offense occurred will be forfeited and the contractor or subcontractor will not receive any further payment.

GUARANTEED ENERGY SAVINGS CONTRACTS

I. GENERAL

A. Applicability

In lieu of utilizing most of the public construction laws described earlier in this Part I, school corporations may choose to enter into a guaranteed energy savings contract for renovation or rehabilitation projects which consist primarily of projects containing energy conservation measures. Indiana law defines an energy conservation measure as "a school facility alteration designed to reduce energy consumption costs or other operating costs...." Examples provided in the statute include (1) providing insulation, (2) installing window or door systems, (3) installing automatic energy control systems, (4) modifying or replacing heating and air conditioning systems, (5)installing lighting fixtures, in certain circumstances, and (6) any facility improvements which reduce future labor costs, costs for contracted services and related capital expenditures. School corporations may also include in the guaranteed energy savings contract process work which is not part of an energy conservation measure as long as (1) the total cost of such work does not exceed fifteen percent of the total cost of the guaranteed energy savings contract, and (2) either (a) the work is necessary to conform to a law, rule or ordinance, or (b) the guaranteed energy savings contract provides evidence that (i) there is an economic advantage in the form of a savings to the school corporation to complete the project as a part of the renovation project, and (ii) the savings is calculated in accordance with industry engineering standards identified in Indiana Code 36-1-12.5, as amended. These conclusions must be reported to the Indiana Department of Commerce.

B. Limitations

1.   The guaranteed energy savings contract must be with a qualified provider. A qualified provider is defined as a person or entity who is (a) experienced in the design, implementation and installation of energy conservation measures, (b) certified by the State of Indiana as a qualified provider of energy conservation measures, (c) providing energy conservation engineering services by a professional engineer licensed by the State of Indiana, (d) providing for the duration of the guarantee under the guaranteed energy savings contract (i) monitoring for the facility performance guarantee and (ii) service personnel under the person's or entity's direct employment and supervision, (e) providing at least twenty percent of the work with its own workforce, and (f) submitting to the school corporation a performance bond to ensure the person's or entity's faithful performance of its obligations over the term of the guaranteed energy savings contract.

2.   A guaranteed energy savings contract may have a term no longer than the lesser of ten years or the average life of the energy conservation measures installed, with the term of the contract beginning on the date of the final installation.

3. A guaranteed energy savings contract must provide (a) the savings in energy and operating costs obtained as a result of installing the energy conservation measures are guaranteed by the qualified provider to cover the costs of such measures, (b) the qualified provider will reimburse the school corporation for the difference between the guaranteed savings and the actual savings (including stipulated savings), and (c) the payments by the school corporation under the guaranteed energy savings contract are (i) subject to annual appropriation by the school board and (ii) not indebtedness of the school corporation. As mentioned in the previous sentence, the actual savings under the guaranteed energy savings contract may be either actual savings, stipulated savings or a combination of actual and stipulated savings. If the school corporation and the qualified provider agree, or stipulate, to deem the occurrence of certain savings under the guaranteed energy savings contract, those stipulated savings must be calculated in accordance with certain industry engineering standards identified in Indiana Code 36-1-12.5, as amended.

II. PROCEDURES

A. Qualified Provider Selection

The first step in entering into a guaranteed energy savings contract is the selection of the qualified provider. This selection process must be done through a public request process in which the school board publishes a notice in one or two newspapers which are either published or generally circulated in the geographical boundaries of the school corporation. This notice must state that the school corporation is requesting qualified providers to propose energy conservation measures through a guaranteed energy savings contract and the date, time and place where such proposals will be received. This notice must be published two times with at least one week between publications and with the second publication being published at least thirty days prior to the date proposals must be submitted. Indiana law does not specify any required form for such proposals. In addition, Indiana law does not provide school corporations with any guidance on how the school board should select the qualified provider among those submitting proposals.

B. Energy Conservation Report

Once the school board selects a qualified provider, the qualified provider must prepare and submit a report to the school board prior to the installation of the energy conservation measures. The report must include (a) an estimate of (i) all costs attributable to the energy conservation measures recommended by the qualified provider and agreed to by the school board, including the costs of design, engineering, intallation, maintenance, repairs and repayment of any financing, and (ii) the amount of energy consumption or operating costs reductions as a result of the installation of the energy conservation measures, and (b) a list of all contractors and subcontractors to be used by the qualified provider with respect to the energy conservation measures.

C. Compliance with other Indiana laws

All guaranteed energy savings contracts must comply with the requirements of Indiana's common construction wage laws. (Refer to "Common Construction Wage Process" in this Part I.) In addition, all energy conservation measures must be approved by the Indiana Department of Health, the Office of the State Fire Marshall and the State Building Commissioner.

D. Annual Report

After the completion of the project, the school board must annually file a report with the Indiana Department of Commerce identifying the savings achieved during the previous year. This annual report must be filed for the term of guaranteed energy savings contract.

III. PAYMENT OF GUARANTEED ENERGY SAVINGS CONTRACTS

A. General Fund

While it is highly unlikely, a school corporation may wish to pay all or a portion of the cost of the guaranteed energy savings contract from the school corporation's general fund. To make such payment, the school corporation would need to make sure an appropriation in the amount of such payment is in the general fund.

B. Capital Projects Fund

Depending on the total cost of the guaranteed energy savings contract and the amount of available money in a school corporation's capital projects fund, a school corporation may choose to pay all or a portion of the cost of the guaranteed energy savings contract from money in its capital projects fund. This would require the school corporation's capital projects plan to either contain projects of the type of the energy conservation measures or be amended to include such projects. In addition, an appropriation for the expenditure of such money for the energy conservation measures would need to be in the school corporation's capital projects fund.

C. Bond/Lease Proceeds

If the energy conservation measures are being done in connection with other projects which are being funded from proceeds of general obligation bonds or a lease with a building corporation, then the school corporation may choose to use a portion of such proceeds to pay for all or a portion of the cost of the guaranteed energy savings contract. All of the procedures of general obligation bonds or building lease financing will apply. (Refer to "General Obligation Bonds" and "Lease Financing" in Part II.)

D. Installment Payment Contract

Installment payment contracts are by far the most common funding method chosen by school corporations. Installment payment contracts are entered into between the qualified provider and the school corporation. The qualified provider usually sells or assigns its interest to a bank or financial institution which in turn provides the qualified provider with money in an amount sufficient to pay the cost of the guaranteed energy savings contract. The school corporation agrees to pay the cost of the guaranteed energy savings contract, together with interest on such amount, in semi-annual payments for a term specified in the installment payment contract, which term may not exceed the lesser of ten years or the average life of the energy conservation measures installed, with the term of the contract beginning on the date of the final installation. Under Indiana law, the school corporation may use money in its general fund or its capital projects fund to make such annual payments. Because Indiana law requires the payments made under installment payment contracts entered into by a school corporation to be subject to annual appropriation, such contracts are not treated as indebtedness of the school corporation. In addition, Indiana law specifically states that Indiana's petition-remonstrance laws do not apply to such contracts.

ACQUISITION AND DISPOSITION OF EQUIPMENT

GENERAL ISSUES FOR THE ACQUISITION OF SUPPLIES

A. Applicability

Any lease or purchase of equipment by, or on behalf of, a school corporation, which is paid from any fund held by the school corporation or from the proceeds of any financing which is repaid, in whole or in part, from funds of the school corporation must comply with Indiana public purchasing laws.

B. Exceptions

1. The Indiana public purchasing laws do not apply to the purchase of equipment between two units of government.

2. The Indiana public purchasing laws do not apply to a public works project which is subject to the Indiana public construction laws.

3. The Indiana public purchasing laws do not apply to any collective bargaining agreement or any other employment relationship between an employee and the school corporation.

4. The Indiana public purchasing laws do not apply to any investment of public funds.

5. The Indiana public purchasing laws do not apply to any contract for social services.

6. The Indiana public purchasing laws do not apply to the acquisition of any equipment in connection with any guaranteed energy savings contract.

7. If equipment is being acquired with money donated to a school corporation, the school corporation does not need to comply with the Indiana public purchasing laws if compliance with the Indiana public purchasing laws would violate the terms and conditions of the gift and invalidate the gift.

C. Purchasing Agencies and Agents

1. The school board is the most common form of purchasing agency for each school corporation. However, some school corporations have entered into agreements with one another to create a purchasing cooperative. The purchasing cooperative designates the person or entity with the authority to conduct all acquisition of equipment by the cooperative members.

2. The purchasing agent is the person authorized by the purchasing agency to act as the agent for the purchasing agency in the administration of the duties of the purchasing agency. A school corporation or purchase cooperative may have more than one purchasing agent. The purchasing agent is responsible for preparing and maintaining

all equipment specifications and managing the administration of acquisition of equipment under the Indiana public purchasing laws.

D. Key Defined Terms

1.   "Purchase" as defined under the Indiana public purchasing laws includes all of the activities of acquiring supplies. Purchase includes either the buying or leasing of supplies.

2.   "Services" as defined under the Indiana public purchasing laws means the furnishing of labor, time or effort by a person, but not including the delivery of specific supplies. The manner in which a school corporation may purchase services is to be determined by the school board, and is not subject to any of the requirements described for the acquisition of supplies.

3.   "Specifications" as defined under the Indiana public purchasing laws means a written document containing the physical or functional characteristics of a certain supply or service, including a description of the requirement for inspecting, testing or preparing such supply or service for delivery to the school corporation. Unless otherwise provided by the Indiana public purchasing laws, school corporations must prepare specifications in connection with the acquisition of all supplies or services. In lieu of preparing specifications, a school board may issue a request for specifications if the purchasing agent makes a written determination that the development of specifications is not feasible. The request for specification must include (a) the factors or criteria that will be used in evaluating the specifications, (b) a statement concerning the relative importance of price and the other evaluation factors, and (c) a statement concerning whether discussions may be conducted with persons proposing specifications to clarify the specification requirements.

4.   "Supplies" as defined under the Indiana public purchasing laws means any property, including, but not limited to, equipment, goods and materials. Supplies do not include any interest in real property.

E. Applicability to the Public Records Laws

In general, contract and purchasing records of the school corporation are public records. However, a school corporation may establish policies for the protection of documents submitted to the school corporation in response to a solicitation for the purpose of (1) protecting offers before opening to prevent disclosure, (2) affording unobstructed evaluation of offers after opening, and (3) protecting offers from tampering both before and after opening.

ACQUISITION & DISPOSITION OF EQUIPMENT

II. COMPETITIVE BIDDING PROCESS FOR THE ACQUISITION OF SUPPLIES

A. General

1. A purchasing agent must generally use competitive bidding in awarding a contract for supplies. The competitive bidding process begins with the publication of an invitation for bids by the purchasing agent. This notice must be published in one or two newspapers published or generally circulated in the geographical boundaries of the school corporation. The notice must be published two times with the publications being at least one week apart and the second publication being at least one week prior to the day bids are to be received. The invitation for bids must include (a) a purchase description, (b) all contractual terms and conditions that apply to the purchase, (c) a statement of the evaluation criteria that will be used, including (inspection, testing, quality, workmanship, delivery, suitability for a particular purpose), (d) the time and place for opening the bids, (e) a statement concerning whether the bid must be accompanied by a certified check or other evidence of financial responsibility, and (f) a statement concerning the conditions under which a bid may be canceled or rejected in whole or in part. All evaluation criteria that will affect the bid price or be considered in the evaluation for an award must be objectively measurable, and only evaluation criteria specified in the invitation for bids may be used in the evaluation of bids received by the school board.

2. The purchasing agency must publicly open bids in the presence of at least one person at the time and place specified in the invitation for bids. Bids must be unconditionally accepted; however, if a bidder inserts contract terms or bids on items not specified in the invitation for bids, the purchasing agent (a) must treat such additional contract terms or bids as a proposal from the bidder as additions to the contract and (b) may (i) declare the bidder nonresponsive, (ii) permit the bidder to withdraw the proposed additions, or (iii) accept any of the proposed additions unless the additions are prejudicial to the interest of the school corporation or fair competition. The contract must be awarded in a reasonably responsive timeframe by written notice to the lowest responsible and responsive bidder. The governmental body may adopt rules or establish policies to allow the correction or withdrawal of an inadvertently erroneous bid before or after award, or policies allowing cancellation of awards based on a mistake. However, the purchasing agency must maintain the name of each bidder and the amount of each bid to be made available to the public after each contract award.

B. Small Business Set-Aside

1. As long as the school corporation reasonably expects that offers will be obtained from at least two small business (as defined in this paragraph) capable of providing the supplies and services at a fair and reasonable price, a school corporation may implement rules in which the solicitation to acquire supplies states that offers for the

supplies will only be accepted from small businesses. The Indiana public purchasing laws define a small business to be a business which (a) is independently owned and operated, (b) is not dominant in the field of operations, and (c) (i) if the business is a wholesale business, does not have annual sales for its most recently completed fiscal year exceeding $4,000,000, (ii) if the business is a construction business does not have average annual receipts for the preceding three fiscal years exceeding $4,000,000, (iii) if the business is a retail business or a business selling services does not have annual sales or receipts exceeding $500,000, or (iv) if the business is a manufacturing business, does not employ more than 100 employees. If a school corporation chooses to implement rules for the acquisition of supplies from small businesses, it must establish criteria for determining any qualifications as a small business which are in addition to those described in this paragraph. In establishing any additional criteria, the rules may use any standards established for determination of small business status which are used by any agency of the federal government. In addition, a school corporation may receive assistance in establishing any additional criteria from the Indiana Department of Commerce. The criteria must provide that when computing the size of an offeror, the annual receipts and sales of the offeror and all affiliates must be included. The small business set-aside designation must be made before the solicitation for purchase is issued and the public notice of the purchase must reflect that the purchase is a small business set-aside.

2. If a contract is awarded, then it should be awarded to the lowest responsible and responsive offeror. However, the purchasing agent may withdraw the small business set-aside and reject all offers if it is determined that acceptance of the lowest responsive and responsible offer will result in the payment of an unreasonable price.

3. This small business set-aside is in addition to the mandatory small business preference described in paragraph C-1 below.

C. Other Purchasing Preferences

1. The acquisition of supplies by a school corporation may qualify for a purchasing preference identified under the Indiana public purchasing laws. The offeror may claim one preference from the following list of preferences: (a) an Indiana business preference adopted by the school corporation, (b) a recycled materials or post-consumer materials preference unless the solicitation is limited to supplies containing recycled materials or post-consumer materials, (c) a soy diesel/bio diesel preference unless the solicitation is limited to fuel containing soy diesel/bio diesel of at least twenty percent by volume, (d) a high calcium food and beverage preference, and (e) a small business preference. While the preference provided under clause (a) is only available if it is adopted by the school board, the preferences described in clauses (b) through and including (e) are mandatory preferences. Each preference has a maximum permitted price difference allowed to offerors providing supplies claiming one of these preferences.

ACQUISITION & DISPOSITION OF EQUIPMENT

2. An offeror who wants to claim a preference provided under the Indiana public purchasing laws must indicate the preference in the offer and state what supply item is the preferred supply. An offeror may claim only one preference among the preferences listed in clauses (b), (c) or (d). A price preference percentage is determined based on the claimed preference, and this percentage is utilized to calculate an adjusted offer. The award of contract is given to the offeror with the lowest adjusted offer.

3. School corporations must acquire supplies manufactured in the United States of America unless the school board determines that (a) the supplies are not manufactured in the United States of America in reasonably available quantities, (b) the price of the supplies manufactured in the United States of America exceeds by an unreasonable amount the price of available and comparable supplies manufactured elsewhere, (c) the quality of the supplies manufactured in the United States of America is substantially less than comparably priced available supplies manufactured elsewhere, or (d) the acquisition of supplies manufactured in the United States in not in the public interest.

4. School corporations must acquire steel products which are manufactured in the United States of America unless the president of the school board determines in writing that (a) this requirement would increase the acquisition cost by more than fifteen percent, and (b) the failure to acquire steel products manufactured in the United States would not in any way (i) harm the business of a facility that manufactures steel products in Indiana, or (ii) result in the reduction of employment or wages and benefits of employees of a facility that manufactures steel products in Indiana. This requirement also does not apply to the acquisition of steel products which are less than $10,000 and made under the small purchase process.

5. School corporations may not award supply contracts for supplies made in a country other than the United States of America if the supplies were made using forced labor.

III. EXCEPTIONS TO THE COMPETITIVE BIDDING PROCESS FOR THE ACQUISITION OF SUPPLIES

A. Small Purchases Exception

For all acquisitions expected to be less than $25,000, the general procedures for competitive bidding described above are not required, and the purchasing agency may establish the procedures and requirements for such acquisitions. For acquisitions expected to be between $25,000 and $75,000, the purchasing agent may, in lieu of the competitive bidding process described above, invite quotes from at least three people or entities known to deal in the supplies to be acquired. The purchasing agent must mail the invitation to quote at least seven days prior to the time fixed to receive quotes. Upon receiving the quotes, the purchasing agent may either reject all quotes or award the contract to the lowest responsible and responsive offeror. If the purchasing agent does not receive a quote from a

PART I: BUILDING PROJECTS

responsible and responsive offeror, the purchasing agent may acquire the supplies under any special purchase method.

B. Request for Proposals Exception

1.   If the purchasing agent makes a written determination that the use of competitive bidding process described above is either not practicable or not advantageous to the school corporation, the purchasing agent may use a request for proposal process in lieu of the competitive bidding process. The request for proposal process involves the publishing of a notice in one or two newspapers which are published or generally circulated in the geographical boundaries of the school corporation. The notice must be published twice at least one week apart with the second publication being at least seven days before the receipt of the proposals. The request for proposals must include (a) the factors or criteria that will be used in evaluating the proposals, (b) a statement concerning the relative importance of price and the other evaluation factors, (c) a statement concerning whether the proposal must be accompanied by a certified check or other evidence of financial responsibility, and (d) a statement concerning whether discussions may be conducted with responsible offerors, who submit proposals determined to be reasonably susceptible of being selected for award.

2.   Unlike the competitive bidding process, proposals must be opened privately so as to avoid disclosure to competing offerors during the negotiation process. Only those factors listed in the request for proposals may be used for evaluation, and award should be made to the responsible offeror whose proposal is determined in writing to be the most advantageous, taking into consideration price and other listed evaluation factors. A register of proposals must be prepared and made available to the public after the contract is awarded. This register must include (a) a copy of the request for proposals, (b) a list of all people or entities to whom the request for proposals was sent, (c) a list of all proposals received (including names and addresses, dollar amount of each offer, and the name of the successful offeror and the dollar amount of that offeror's offer), (d) the basis on which the award was made, and (e) the entire contents of the contract file except for proprietary information included with an offer.

C. Special Purchasing Methods

1.   Under certain circumstances, purchases may be made without complying with the competitive bidding, the small purchase or request for proposals processes. However, Indiana law requires that effort be made to preserve competition in any acquisition process if practicable. If a special purchase is made, the purchasing agent will maintain the contract records in a separate file. In the file, there must be a written determination of (a) the basis for using the special purchase exception and (b) the selection of the contractor. A record including each contractor's name, the amount and type of each contract, and a description of the supplies purchased must be maintained for a minimum of at least five years.

ACQUISITION & DISPOSITION OF EQUIPMENT

2. Special purchases may be made (a) where there exists under emergency conditions, a threat to public heath, welfare, or safety, (b) where there exists a unique opportunity for substantial savings, (c) at an auction, (d) for the purchase of data processing contracts or license agreements for (i) software programs or (ii) supplies or services where only one source meets the school corporation's reasonable requirements, (e) when the compatibility of equipment, accessories or replacement parts is a substantial consideration in the acquisition and only one source meets the school corporation's reasonable requirements, (f) when using the competitive bidding, small purchase or request for proposals process would seriously impair the functioning of the school corporation, (g) when the purchasing agency has used the competitive bidding, small purchase or request for proposals process and not received a responsive offer, (h) when the purchasing agent is attempting to evaluate supplies for the purpose of (i) obtaining functional information or comparative data, or (ii) advancing the long term competitive position of the school corporation, (i) when the market structure of the supplies are based on price but the school corporation is able to receive a dollar or percentage discount of the established price, (j) when there is only one source for the supply and the purchasing agent determines in writing there is only one source for the supply, (k) when the purchasing agent determines in writing that (i) supplies can be acquired at prices equal to or less than the prices stipulated in the current federal supply service schedules established by the General Services Administration, and (ii) it is advantageous to the school corporation's interest in efficiency and economy, (l) from a person or entity who has a contract with a federal agency and the person's or entity's contract requires the person or entity to make the supplies available to the local units of government, (m) from a person or entity who has a contract with a state agency and the person's or entity's contract requires the person or entity to make the supplies available to the local units of government, (n) from the federal government if the purchasing agent determines that the acquisition will cost less than the cost of the supplies through the competitive bidding, small purchase or request for proposals processes, provided, however, notice of such acquisition must be published by the purchasing agent at the time or immediately after such acquisition, and the notice must be published one time in one or two newspapers generally circulated or published in the geographical boundaries of the school corporation, (o) when accepting a gift, (p) for the purchase of supplies from a public utility as long as the acquisition price takes into account the results of an independent appraisal obtained by the school board and the results of an independent appraisal obtained by the public utility, or (q) for the purchase of supplies at a fair market price from a nonprofit agency for persons with severe disabilities which (i) complies with the Indiana laws governing private nonprofit organizations, (ii) is certified by the Wage and Hour Division of the United States Department of Labor, (iii) meets the standards adopted by the Secretary of the Indiana Department of Family and Social Services, and (iv) files the reports required under Indiana Code § 16-32-2-7, as amended.

IV. REQUIRED PURCHASES

A. Purchases from the Department of Corrections

If supplies and services (1) meet the specifications and needs of the school corporation and (2) can be purchased from the Indiana Department of Correction at a fair market price, the school corporation is required to purchase such supplies from the Indiana Department of Correction in lieu of using the competitive bidding, small purchase or request for proposals processes unless the supplies and services cannot be furnished in a timely manner.

B. Purchase of Rehabilitation Center Products

If supplies and services (1) meet the specifications and needs of the school corporation and (2) can be purchased from the Indiana Rehabilitation Services Bureau of the Division of Disability, Aging and Rehabilitative Services at a fair market price, the school corporation is required to purchase such supplies from the Indiana Rehabilitation Services Bureau of the Division of Disability, Aging and Rehabilitative Services in lieu of using the competitive bidding, small purchase or request for proposals processes unless the supplies and services cannot be furnished in a timely manner.

V. QUALIFICATIONS AND DUTIES OF OFFERORS AND PROSPECTIVE CONTRACTORS FOR THE ACQUISITION OF SUPPLIES

A. General

Offerors must be determined to be responsible and responsive to be awarded a contract under the Indiana public purchasing laws.

B. Responsible Offerors

1. If a purchasing agent determines an offeror is not responsible, that determination must be made in writing by the purchasing agent. If an offeror fails to provide information required by the purchasing agent concerning a determination of whether the offeror is responsible, that offeror may not be considered responsible under the Indiana public purchasing laws.

2. Information furnished by an offeror in order to show the offeror is responsible may not be disclosed outside the board and administration of the school corporation without the offeror's prior written consent.

3. In determining whether an offeror is responsible, a purchasing agent may consider (a) the ability and capacity of the offeror to provide the supplies or service solicited, (b) the integrity, character, and reputation of the offeror, and (c) the competency and experience of the offeror. A purchasing agent may also specify in a solicitation that an offeror must provide evidence of financial responsibility to be considered responsible. This evidence may be in the form of a bond, certified check, or other evidence specified in the solicitation. If a bond or certified check is required by

ACQUISITION & DISPOSITION OF EQUIPMENT

the purchasing agent, the amount of the bond or certified check may not be for an amount which is in excess of ten percent of the acquisition price and should be made payable to the school corporation. The check of the successful offeror must be held until delivery or completion of the contract.

4. If an offeror is a foreign corporation, it also must be registered with the Indiana Secretary of State to do business in Indiana in order to be considered responsible. The purchasing agent may award a contract to an offeror pending the offeror's registration with the Indiana Secretary of State. If after a reasonable period time in the judgment of the purchasing agent, the offeror has not registered with the Indian Secretary of State, the purchasing agent must cancel the contract, and the offeror has no cause of action regarding such cancellation.

5. The Indiana public purchasing laws allow for the prequalification of contractors for particular types of supplies.

C. Responsive Offerors

1. In determining whether an offeror is responsive, the purchasing agent may consider (a) whether the offeror has submitted an offer that conforms in all material respects to the specifications, (b) whether the offeror has submitted an offer that complies specifically with the solicitation and the instructions to offerors, and (c) whether the offeror has complied with all applicable statutes, ordinances, resolutions, or rules pertaining to the award of a public contract.

2. In addition, an offeror must file with the purchasing agent, under the penalties of perjury, a non-collusion affidavit, which provides the offeror has not entered into a combination or agreement (a) relative to the price to be offered by a person or entity, (b) to prevent any person or entity from making an offer, or (c) to induce any person or entity to refrain from making an offer. The purchasing agent must reject any offer which the purchasing agents finds to be collusive. If after awarding the contract, the purchasing agent discovers that the successful offeror's affirmation was false, the purchasing agent must declare the contract forfeited and award a new contract. A person convicted of perjury for filing a false affirmation under the Indiana public purchasing laws may not be a party to a contract under the Indiana public purchasing laws for three years following the date of the conviction.

VI. AWARDING CONTRACTS AND CONTRACT TERMS FOR THE ACQUISITION OF SUPPLIES

A. Cost-based Contracts

A school corporation may not enter into contract in which the supplier is compensated based on a cost of the supplies plus a percentage of cost contract. However, a school corporation may enter into a contract for supplies which is a cost reimbursement contract, if the purchasing agent determines in writing that this type of contract is likely to be

PART I: BUILDING PROJECTS

less costly to the school corporation than any other contract type, or that it is impracticable to obtain supplies otherwise.

B. Duration, Renewal, Payment, and Performance Obligations

1. Under the Indiana public purchasing laws the term of a contract for supplies may not exceed four years unless the contract is for the remediation of hazardous waste as defined in the Indiana public purchasing laws. For hazardous waste contracts the term of the contract may not exceed ten years.

2. A contract that contains a provision for escalation of the price of the contract may be renewed if the price escalation is computed using (a) a commonly accepted index named in the contract, or (b) a formula set forth in the contract. A contract may be renewed any number of times by the parties, but the term of the renewed contract may not be any longer than the term of the original contract.

3. In addition, the contract must specify that the payment and performance obligations of the school corporation are subject to the appropriation and availability of funds. Prior to awarding the contract, the school corporation must have available a sufficient appropriation balance or an approved additional appropriation. When the school board makes a written determination that funds are not appropriated or otherwise available to support the continued performance by the school corporation of the contract, the contract is considered canceled. This determination is final and conclusive.

4. If included in the solicitation, the purchasing agent may specify in a contract that early performance or late completion of the contract will result in increased/decreased compensation at either (a) a percentage of the contract amount, or (b) a specified dollar amount.

5. Contracts for the purchase of petroleum products (gasoline, fuel oils, lubricants and liquid asphalt) may allow for the escalation or de-escalation of price, and may be awarded to either the lowest responsible and responsive offeror, or to all responsible and responsive offerors. If the contract is awarded to all responsible and responsive offerors, then the school corporation must purchase the petroleum products identified in the solicitation from the lowest responsible and responsive offeror until the lowest responsible and responsive offeror notifies the school corporation of any change in the price of the petroleum products. Under the Indiana public purchasing laws, the terms of the contract with the lowest responsible and responsive offeror must require that the offeror provide five business days written notice to the school corporation of any such change in price. Upon receipt of notice, the purchasing agent must request current price quotes in writing based upon terms and conditions of the original offer (as awarded) from all successful responsible and responsive offerors. Upon receiving such written quotes, the purchasing agent must then purchase the petroleum from the lowest responsible and responsive offeror, taking into account the price change of the current supplier and the price quotes of the other responsible

and responsive offerors.

6. A solicitation may provide that offers will be received and contracts will be awarded separately. However, if the solicitation does not indicate how separate contracts might be awarded, then the purchasing agent must make a written determination showing that the award of separate contracts is in the interest of efficiency and economy. Similarly, if a purchasing agent awards a contract to an offeror who is other than the lowest offeror, then the purchasing agent must make a written determination stating the reasons for awarding a contract to that offeror.

7. A solicitation may provide that the purchasing agent will award a contract for supplies for an unspecified number of items at a fixed price per unit. Such a contract may include a formula or a method for the escalation of the unit price.

C. Cancellation of Solicitation or Rejection of Offers

A purchasing agent may cancel a solicitation or reject all offers if the purchasing determines in writing such action is in the best interests of the school corporation. Such written determination must be made a part of the contract file.

D. Delay of the Opening of Offers

A school corporation may delay the opening of all offers from the time and date established in the solicitation if (1) the school corporation makes a written determination that the delay is in the best interest of the school corporation, and (2) the day, time and place of the rescheduled opening is announced at the day, time and place of the originally scheduled opening.

E. Determinations

1. All determinations made by a school corporation under the Indiana public purchasing laws are final and conclusive and subject to judicial review. An Indiana court will grant relief only if it determines that a person or entity seeking judicial relief has been substantially prejudiced by a determination that is (a) arbitrary, capricious, an abuse of discretion or otherwise not in accordance with law, (b) contrary to constitutional rights, power, privilege or immunity, (c) in excess of statutory jurisdiction, authority or limitations or short of statutory right, (d) without observance of procedure required by law, or (e) unsupported by substantial evidence. The burden of demonstrating the invalidity of the determination is upon the person or entity asserting such invalidity. Upon a finding that a person or entity has been substantially prejudiced by a determination, a court may set aside the determination by the school corporation or remand the case to the school corporation for further proceedings. However, a court may not award any damages to any aggrieved person or entity.

2.   Additionally, the Indiana public purchasing laws grants the right of any Indiana taxpayer to (a) challenge any determination made on the requirement under the Indiana public purchasing laws to use steel manufactured in the United States, or (b) enforce the requirement under the Indiana public purchasing laws to use steel manufactured in the United States.

F. **Political Subdivision Filing for Public Record and Inspection**

Within thirty days after acceptance of an offer, the purchasing agent must deliver in person or by first class mail to the successful offeror the original of each purchase order or lease, retain a copy for the purchasing agent's records, and file a copy for public record and inspection with the records of the school corporation.

G. **Modification and Termination Of Contracts**

1.   A school corporation may establish policies or adopt rules for the inclusion of contract clauses (a) concerning adjustments in contract prices or time of performance, (b) allowing the school corporation the unilateral right to order, in writing, changes in the work within the scope of the contract or temporary stopping of the work, or (c) allowing for variations between estimated quantities of work in a contract and actual quantities.

2.   Any contract terms which allow for adjustments in price must be calculated (a) by agreement on a fixed price adjustment before the beginning of the performance of the contract or as soon as practicable after the beginning of such performance, (b) by unit prices specified in the contract or subsequently agreed upon, (c) by the costs attributable to the events or situations under the clauses in the contract governing adjustment in price with adjustment of the profit or fee as specified in the contract or as subsequently agreed upon by the parties, (d) by such other manner as is mutually agreeable to the parties, or (e) by a unilateral determination by the school board of the costs attributable to the events or situations under the clauses in the contract which govern adjustments in price with adjustment of the profit or fee being computed by the school board in accordance with the rules adopted by the school board.

VII.   DISPOSITION OF SURPLUS PROPERTY

A. **General**

A purchasing agent may sell (1) property that has been left in the custody of an officer or employee of the school corporation and has remained unclaimed for more than one year, or (2) property that is no longer needed or is unfit for the purpose for which it was intended. Notice of any sale of surplus property must be published in one or two newspapers generally circulated or published in the geographical boundaries of the school corporation. This notice must be published twice with at least one week between each publication and the second publication being at least fifteen days before the date of sale. If the property to be

ACQUISITION & DISPOSITION OF EQUIPMENT

sold is one item with an estimated value of more than $1,000, or more than one item with an estimated total value of $5,000 or more, then the purchasing agent may engage an auctioneer to advertise the sale and conduct a public auction. The advertising must include a detailed description of the property to be sold, and the purchasing agency must pay the auctioneer from the gross proceeds of the sale before other expenses are paid. The school corporation may also sell the surplus property using an internet auction site that is (1) approved by the Indiana Intelenet Commission and (2) linked to the electronic gateway administered by the Indiana Intelenet Commission. The posting of the sale on the internet auction site must include a detailed description of the surplus property to be sold. The purchasing agency may pay the costs of conducting the auction on the internet sites as required by the person or entity maintaining the auction site. If an auctioneer is not engaged, or the surplus property is not sold through an internet auction site, then the school corporation must sell the property at a public sale or by sealed bids. All sales must be made to the highest responsible bidder.

B. Exceptions

1. If the value of one item being sold is less than $1,000, or more than one item with an estimated total value of less than $5,000, then the school corporation may sell the property at a public or private sale, or transfer the property without advertising.

2. If the property to be sold is material which may be recycled or has been collected by a recycling program, then the school corporation does not need to advertise the sale or transfer of the property.

3. Worthless property may be demolished or junked and is not required to be sold. Property may be considered worthless if the value of the property is less than the estimated costs of the sale and transportation of the property.

4. A school corporation may exchange property with another unit of government upon terms and condition to exchange property acceptable to the parties. These transfers may be made for any amount of property or cash as agreed upon by the parties.

PART II

BORROWING

GENERAL OBLIGATION BONDS • LEASE FINANCING • MISCELLANEOUS FINANCING METHODS • PETITION – REMONSTRANCE PROCESS

GENERAL OBLIGATION BONDS

I. GENERAL

A. Definition

Under Indiana law, general obligation bonds include any obligation issued by a school corporation, except tax anticipation warrants, installment payment contracts used to finance guaranteed energy savings projects, bus loans and certain short-term limited recourse obligations.

B. Uses

School corporations may issue bonds to fund land acquisition, construction and/or renovation projects, equipment purchases, school bus purchases, court judgments and all incidental expenses incurred in connection with the bond issue.

C. Maturity Date

General obligation bonds issued for the funding of judgments or for the purchase of school buses cannot having a maturity exceeding five years, and general obligation bonds issued for all other purposes cannot have a maturity exceeding twenty-five years.

D. Debt Limitation

The aggregate outstanding principal amount of all general obligation bonds of a school corporation may not exceed two percent of one-third of the true tax value of the school corporation. Any general obligation bonds in excess of this amount are void. This rule does not apply to general obligation pension bonds. However, the outstanding principal amount of general obligation pension bonds is taken into account when determining the ability to issue general obligation bonds for other purposes.

II. ISSUANCE PROCEDURES

A. 1028 Process

If a school corporation anticipates spending more than $1,000,000 in connection with a construction, renovation or expansion project, it must hold a public hearing on the project. This hearing is commonly referred to as the "1028 Public Hearing." (Refer to "Building Projects -- Public Construction" in Part I.)

B. Local Approval Process

1. In all general obligation bond issues, there are four local approval steps which are usually taken by a school board in connection with the issuance of general obligation bonds. Those steps are: (a) the adoption of a preliminary bond resolution; (b) the convening of a public hearing on the appropriation of the proceeds of the bonds; (c)

the adoption of an additional appropriation resolution; and (d) the adoption of a final bond resolution. The adoption of a preliminary bond resolution is usually the first step taken in the approval process and if it is financing a project which is anticipated to cost more than $1,000,000, it is usually adopted at the conclusion of the 1028 Public Hearing. Sometime prior to the issuance of the bonds, the school board must hold the additional appropriation public hearing. The notice for this hearing must be published at least ten days prior to the hearing. Following the hearing, the school board may adopt the additional appropriation resolution and instruct the treasurer of the school corporation to file a report of additional appropriation with the State Department of Local Government Finance. The final step in the local approval process is the adoption by the school board of the final bond resolution. This is usually adopted after receiving approval of the bond issue by the State Department of Local Government Finance, and before receiving the bids on the bonds.

2.   If a bond issue is financing a controlled project as defined under Indiana Code § 6-1.1-20, as amended, a school corporation must also go through all or a portion of the petition-remonstrance process. (Refer to "Petition - Remonstrance Process" later in this Part II.)

C. State Approval Process

All general obligation bond issues must be approved by the State Department of Local Government Finance. To receive this approval, the school corporation files a petition with the State Department of Local Government Finance for approval to issue the general obligation bonds. The Commissioner of the State Department of Local Government Finance, who is appointed by the Governor of the State of Indiana, most always refers the matter to the School Property Tax Control Board for review. The School Property Tax Control Board serves as an advisory body to the Commissioner of the State Department of Local Government Finance, and is comprised of between seven and eleven members. State entities which appoint members to the School Property Tax Control Board are the Governor of the State of Indiana, the State Board of Accounts, the State Department of Local Government Finance, the President Pro Tempore of the Indiana Senate and the Speaker of the Indiana House of Representatives. If the matter is referred to the School Property Tax Control Board, the school corporation will appear at a hearing of the School Property Tax Control Board. At the conclusion of the hearing, the School Property Tax Control Board by a majority vote will (a) recommend the Commissioner of the State Department of Local Government Finance approve the request to issue the general obligation bonds, (b) recommend the Commissioner of the State Department of Local Government Finance deny the request to issue the general obligation bonds, or (c) table the request for further review. Following the receipt of the School Property Tax Control Board's recommendation, the Commissioner of the State Department of Local Government Finance will issue an order regarding this matter. The Commissioner of the State Department of Local Government Finance may accept or reject the recommendation of the School Property Tax Control Board in making its final determination. An appeal of the order of the Commissioner of the State Department of Local Government Finance must be filed with the Indiana State Tax Court no later than thirty days after the order is issued.

GENERAL OBLIGATION BONDS

D. Sale Process

1. All general obligation bonds must be sold through the public sale method unless they are sold to the Indiana Bond Bank, a local public improvement bond bank, the federal government or any agency of the federal government. Under Indiana law the public sale method may be through the publication of either a notice of sale or a notice of intent to sell.

2. The notice of sale method requires the notice to be published in one or two newspapers which are either published or circulated in the school corporation. This notice provides a general description of the terms of the general obligation bonds such as the bond repayment schedule and the prepayment terms and the date and time by which each potential purchaser of the general obligation bonds must submit a bid containing interest rates for each maturity of the bonds and the purchase price to be paid by the potential purchaser. This notice must be published twice with at least one week between the first and second publication. In addition, the first publication must be at least fifteen days before the sale date, and the second publication must be at least three days before the sale date. On the date and time identified in the notice, the superintendent of the school corporation, the assistant superintendent for financial affairs of the school corporation, the business manager or the financial advisor for the school corporation will receive all of the bids, tabulate the bids to determine which bidder is offering the lowest net interest cost on the general obligation bonds, and then award the sale of the general obligation bonds to the bidder who offered the lowest net interest cost on the general obligation bonds. The net interest cost on the general obligation bonds is determined by computing the total interest on all of the general obligation bonds from the date of sale to the date of maturity and deducting from this amount the premium bid, if any, or adding to this amount any discount.

3. The notice of intent to sell method requires the notice to be published in one or two newspapers which are either published or circulated in the school corporation. In addition, the notice must be published in a newspaper which circulates in Indianapolis. This notice provides a general description of the terms of the general obligation bonds such as the bond repayment schedule and the prepayment terms and a statement that by a certain date and time identified in the notice any person interested in submitting a bid for the general obligation bonds must provide in writing to the school corporation official or representative listed in the notice the name, address, telephone number and facsimile number of the potential purchaser. This notice must be published twice with at least one week between the first and second publication. In addition, the second publication must be at least seven days prior to the deadline for potential purchasers to submit their written interest to bid on the general obligation bonds. At least twenty-four hours prior to the sale of the general obligation bonds, the school corporation's official or representative will notify all the interested potential purchasers of the date and time by which all bids on the general obligation bonds must be received by the school corporation's officer

or representative. On the date and time identified in the twenty-four hour notice, the school corporation's official or representative will receive all of the bids, tabulate the bids to determine which bidder is offering the lowest net interest cost on the general obligation bonds, and then award the sale of the general obligation bonds to the bidder who offered the lowest net interest cost on the general obligation bonds. The net interest cost on the general obligation bonds is determined by computing the total interest on all of the general obligation bonds from the date of sale to the date of maturity and deducting from this amount the premium bid, if any, or adding to this amount any discount.

E. Execution Process

All general obligation bonds must be executed in the name and on behalf of the school corporation by the president and secretary of the school board. If all or any of the school board officers cease to be officers for any reason after they have executed the general obligation bonds but before the general obligation bonds have been delivered to the purchaser or purchasers, the general obligation bonds are binding and valid obligations just as if the officers were in office at the time of delivery.

F. Payment Process

To provide for the payment of principal and interest, the governing body must levy an annual tax sufficient to pay the principal and interest as they become due. The State Department of Local Government Finance is required to annually review the tax levy in a school corporation's debt service fund to determine whether such levy is sufficient to pay the principal and interest of the general obligation bonds together with all other payments made out the debt service fund. In addition, if a school corporation fails to pay any of the principal or interest on the general obligation bonds, the Treasurer of the State of Indiana is required to (a) intercept the money provided by the State of Indiana to the school corporation in an amount equal to the unpaid principal and/or interest which is due, and (b) forward the intercepted money to the holder or holders of the general obligation bonds who are owed the money. This is known as the "State Intercept Mechanism," and it has been used on at least one occasion.

G. Expenditure Process

Upon the issuance of the general obligation bonds, the school corporation will deposit the proceeds of the general obligation bonds into a school corporation construction fund (Account Number 070), and pay the costs of the project from the money deposited into that fund and the interest earned on that money. Any money deposited into a school corporation construction fund is subject to the same appropriation and claims procedures as any other fund of the school corporation, including an appropriation public hearing. Because the school corporation construction fund only receives non-property tax funds, however, the school corporation must only file a report of appropriation with the State Department of Local Government Finance, and no approval by the State Department of Local Government Finance of the appropriation is required.

II. OPPOSITION METHODS AVAILABLE

A. Petition-Remonstrance Process

One way to challenge the proposed issuance of general obligation bonds is through the petition-remonstrance process. (Refer to "Petition - Remonstrance Process" later in this Part II.)

B. Objection Process

Another way that taxpayers can challenge the issuance of general obligation bonds is through the objection process. Under Indiana law, following the adoption by the school board of the preliminary bond resolution approving the issuance of bonds to finance a controlled project, the school corporation must publish a notice of its determination to issue general obligation bonds. This notice must be published twice at least one week apart. In addition, this notice must be posted in three public places. The objection process is triggered upon the occurrence of ten or more taxpayers, who own property in the school corporation, filing a petition in the office of the county auditor stating they object to the issuance of the general obligation bonds on the grounds that it is unnecessary or excessive. The petition must be filed within fifteen days after the second publication of the notice of determination is published. When the taxpayers file the petition of objection, the county auditor will forward a certified copy of the petition and any other relevant information to the State Department of Local Government Finance. Within thirty days after receiving the objection petition, the State Department of Local Government Finance will hold a special hearing at a location in the school corporation, at which time objectors and supporters of the general obligation bond issue and the project present evidence and testimony to the representative or representatives of the State Department of Local Government Finance. Following this special hearing, the Commissioner of the State Department of Local Government Finance will issue an order which either denies or accepts the objection petition. An appeal of the order of the Commissioner of the State Department of Local Government Finance must be filed with the Indiana State Tax Court no later than thirty days after the order is issued.

C. Challenge of Validity

Finally, taxpayers can oppose the issuance of general obligation bonds by challenging the validity of the general obligation bonds in a court of law. An action to contest the validity of the general obligation bonds must be brought within fifteen days after the first publication of notice of the sale of general obligation bonds. After the sale of the general obligation bonds, an action to contest the validity of the general obligation bonds must be brought within five days after the bond sale.

LEASE FINANCING

I. GENERAL

A. Background

As discussed earlier in this Part II in the Section entitled "General Obligation Bonds," school corporations may borrow money for construction or renovation projects by issuing general obligation bonds payable from a portion of the annual property taxes collected and distributed to the school corporation. However, a school corporation's ability to issue such bonds is limited by the Indiana Constitution, which prohibits school corporations and other local governmental units from incurring debt in excess of two percent of the assessed valuation of the taxable property within its boundaries. This has been further restricted by an Indiana statute which reduces the formula to two percent of one-third of the true tax value of the taxable property within its boundaries.

To avoid running afoul of these debt limitations, school corporations often decide to finance construction and renovation projects through first mortgage bonds issued by a building corporation or other lessor type entity. The principal and interest payments due on these first mortgage bonds are paid from lease rentals paid by the school corporation to the building corporation in accordance with a lease. Because the first mortgage bonds are issued by the building corporation, they are not treated as debt of the school corporation which is subject to any debt limitation. Because the lease only requires the school corporation to pay if the building or buildings subject to the lease are able to be used and occupied by the school corporation, the lease is not treated as debt of the school corporation, but rather is treated like a current operating expense like utility expenses, insurance premiums and salaries of teachers and staff.

While any entity, including, but not limited to, an individual, for-profit public corporation and nonprofit public building corporation, is permitted under Indiana law to serve as a lessor, the most common entity used for lease financings is the nonprofit public building corporation. Therefore, for the remainder of this Section, we will focus on a lease financing between a school corporation, as the lessee, and a nonprofit public building corporation, as the lessor.

B. The Attributes of the Nonprofit Public Building Corporation

1. These corporations are created with documents prepared by the school corporation's bond counsel and local attorney.

2. This public building corporation will be incorporated and operate as a nonprofit public benefit corporation under Indiana Code 23-17.

3. All of the financing and construction documents, including the lease, the trust indenture and all the construction contracts, should delegate to the school corporation any and all responsibilities and decisions of the nonprofit public building

corporation regarding the project which the nonprofit public building corporation would otherwise have as an owner and lessor of property.

4. The members of the board of directors of the public building corporation will serve on a voluntary basis and will not be compensated for serving on this board.

5. Even though the board of directors of the public building corporation will delegate all of the responsibility concerning the proposed project to the school corporation, the school corporation should include them as insureds under the school corporation's E and O liability policy to ensure that these volunteers will not incur any expenses for being joined with the school corporation in a lawsuit concerning the project.

6. The Articles of Incorporation of the public building corporation will provide that the corporation is organized solely for the purpose of assisting the school corporation with the financing of its school facilities through the acquisition and owning in fee simple of an existing school building or buildings and the land upon which such is located, the acquisition and owning in fee simple of a site or sites appropriate for a new school building or buildings, constructing and equipping a suitable school building or buildings on such site or sites, renovating or expanding an existing school building or buildings, and leasing the same to the school corporation or its successor school corporation, collecting the rentals therefor and applying the proceeds thereof in a manner consistent with Indiana Code 21-5-9 and/or Indiana Code 21-5-12, entirely without profit to the public building corporation, its officers, directors, or incorporators, other than the return of capital actually invested.

7. Because the board of directors serve on a voluntary basis, they will not invest any capital into the public building corporation.

8. All of the costs incurred through the operation of the public building corporation, including the annual filing at the Indiana Secretary of State's Office and all professional fees associated with such operations will be paid by the school corporation or from the proceeds of the bonds.

9. With respect to meetings, the board of directors will have an initial meeting to approve the Articles of Incorporation, the Code of By-Laws, elect officers and approve the form of the Lease with the school corporation. These Articles of Incorporation, Code of By-Laws and officers will be approved by the school board in a formal resolution. In addition, these governing documents of the building corporation provide that the school board is the entity which appoints and removes all of the members of the board of directors of the building corporation and no amendments to these governing documents can be made without the approval of a majority of the school board.

10. Following this meeting, the board of directors will have one to two more meetings within the next six months to a year which will be held in connection with matters related to the proposed bond issue.

11. After the bonds are issued, the board of directors will have one brief meeting each year to sign the annual filing with the Indiana Secretary of State's Office.

12. All of the meetings of the public building corporation will be subject to the same Open Door Law requirements as the meetings of the school board (i.e., posting of meetings and agenda and notification of the media 48 hours prior to the meeting).

C. School Building Defined

The term "school building" includes any building used as a part of or in connection with the operation of a school corporation and includes the site, the landscaping, walks, drives, and playgrounds, except that no building may be constructed with a lease by a building corporation which is designed for and to be used exclusively for interschool athletic contests.

II. PROCEDURES

A. Local Approval Process

1. 1028 Process. If a school corporation anticipates spending more than $1,000,000 in connection with a construction, renovation or expansion project, it must hold a public hearing on the project. This hearing is commonly referred to as the "1028 Public Hearing." (Refer to "Building Projects – Public Construction in Part I.)

2. Petition-Remonstrance Process. If a lease is financing a controlled project as defined under Indiana Code § 6-1.1-20, as amended, a school corporation must also go through all or a portion of the petition-remonstrance process. (Refer to "Petition-Remonstrance Process" later in this Part II.)

3. Lease Process.

   (a) After completion of the 1028 Process and the Petition-Remonstrance Process, if applicable, the school corporation must receive lease petitions signed by at least fifty patrons stating a need for the project exists and the school board needs to investigate entering into a lease with a building corporation to finance the cost of such project. While Indiana law implies that these petitions are initiated by people within the school corporation, in reality these lease petitions are created by the school corporation's bond counsel, and circulated by school board members and other people affiliated with the school corporation. In addition, because it is difficult under Indiana law to determine who is a patron in the school corporation, it is common for these lease petitions to be circulated primarily among owners of real property, which are then verified by the county auditor.

   (b) On or before the meeting at which the school board receives the verified lease petitions, the nonprofit public building corporation approves its

PART II: BORROWING

corporate documents, appoints officers and approves the form of the lease between the school corporation and the building corporation to be used to finance the project.

(c) After the lease has been approved by the building corporation, the school board will receive the verified lease petitions and approve the lease and the design drawings and cost estimates for the project.

(d) After the school board has approved the lease and the design drawings and costs estimates for the project, the school board must hold a public hearing on the lease and the project. Publication of the notice of this public hearing must be published one time in one or two newspapers which are published or circulated in the boundaries of the school corporation. The notice of the public hearing should name the day, place, and hour of the hearing as well as a brief summary of the principal terms of the lease. If the project is the construction of a new school, then the notice of the public hearing must be published at least ten days prior to the date of the public hearing. If the project is the renovation or expansion of an existing school building, then the notice of the public hearing must be published at least thirty days prior to the date of the public hearing. The proposed lease, drawings, plans, specifications, and estimates for the school building must be available for inspection by the public from the date the notice of the public hearing is published until the date of the public hearing. At the public hearing on the lease, the school board must provide the public with the opportunity to comment on the necessity of the lease and whether the rental payments are fair and reasonable. At the conclusion of the public hearing, the school board may (i) confirm the form of lease as originally approved, (ii) modify the lease, but not in any way which increases the lease rentals above the amount described in the public hearing notice, and approve the modified form of the lease, or (iii) reject the lease.

(e) After receiving approval of the lease from the State Department of Local Government Finance, the school corporation and the building corporation execute the lease and publish notice of the execution of the lease. The notice of execution of the least must be published one time in one or two newspapers published or circulated in the boundaries of the school corporation. This triggers a 30-day objection period. (See "Opposition Methods Available--Objection Process" below for more discussion of the objection process.) If no objecting petition is filed, then the building corporation can proceed with the issuance of the first mortgage bonds and the project. While a portion of the first mortgage bond proceeds are paid to the school corporation in connection with the purchase of the land as described in more detail below, most of the proceeds remain with the building corporation under a trust indenture. The funds held under the trust indenture are disbursed by a bank serving as a trustee. The trustee will only disburse such funds when it receives approval for such disbursements from the authorized representative of the building corporation who is usually the superintendent, the assistant superintendent and/or the business manager of the school corporation. Because the funds held by the trustee are not funds of the school corporation, the appropriation and claims procedures do not apply to these payments. However, most school officials receive school board approval of these payments prior to authorization of such payments to make sure the school board agrees and understands the amount of such payments and to whom such payments are being made.

B. Land Purchase Process

Under Indiana law, the building corporation is required to acquire the property on which the school building subject to lease is, or will be, located. To purchase this land, the school corporation must have this property and any buildings currently located on this property appraised. The school corporation may not sell the land to the building corporation for less than appraised fair market value established by the three appraisers; provided, however, if the property was purchased by the school corporation within three years from the sale to the building corporation, then the school corporation may not sell the property for less than the amount paid by the school corporation. However, unlike the normal sale of land by the school corporation which requires the appraisers to be licensed under Indiana law, the appraisers for sales in a lease financing have to only be disinterested owners of real property in the school corporation. In addition, these disinterested owners are not appointed by the school corporation. Instead, these appraisers are appointed by the circuit court of the county in which the school corporation is located.

At the time the first mortgage bonds are issued, the building corporation uses a portion of those first mortgage bond proceeds to pay the school corporation the purchase price of the land and buildings. The school corporation deposits this money in a school corporation construction fund (Account Number 070), and uses that money to fund the portion of the project costs not paid by the building corporation. Any money deposited into a school corporation construction fund is subject to the same appropriation and claims procedures as any other fund of the school corporation, including an appropriation public hearing. Because the school corporation construction fund only receives non-property tax funds, however, the school corporation must only file a report of appropriation with the State Department of Local Government Finance, and no approval by the State Department of Local Government Finance of the appropriation is required.

If a portion of the proceeds of the sale of the real property and buildings received by the school corporation are in connection with an existing building which will be subject to the lease but not renovated or expanded, then the portion of the proceeds received from the sale of that existing building must be spent on the project within one year or transferred to the school corporation's debt service fund.

C. State Approval Process

All leases with a term of longer than five years must be approved by the State Department of Local Government Finance. To receive this approval, the school corporation files a petition with the State Department of Local Government Finance for approval to execute the lease. The Commissioner of the State Department of Local Government Finance, who is appointed by the Governor of the State of Indiana, most always refers the matter to the School Property Tax Control Board for review. The School Property Tax Control Board serves as an advisory body to the Commissioner of the State Department of Local Government Finance, and is comprised of between seven and eleven members. State entities which appoint members to the School Property Tax Control Board are the Governor of the State of Indiana, the State Board of Accounts, the State Department of Local Government Finance, the President Pro Tempore of the Indiana Senate and the Speaker of the Indiana House of Representatives. If the matter is referred to the School Property Tax Control Board, the school corporation will appear at a hearing of the School Property Tax Control Board. At the conclusion, the School Property Tax Control Board by a majority vote will (1) recommend the Commissioner of the State Department of Local Government Finance approve the request to execute the lease, (2) recommend the Commissioner of the State Department of Local Government Finance deny the request to execute the lease, or (3) table the request for further review. Following the receipt of the School Property Tax Control Board's recommendation, the Commissioner of the State Department of Local Government Finance will issue an order regarding this matter. The Commissioner of the State Department of Local Government Finance may accept or reject the recommendation of the School Property Tax Control Board in making its final determination. An appeal of the order of the Commissioner of the State Department of Local Government Finance must be filed with the Indiana State Tax Court no later than thirty days after the order is issued.

D. Payment Process

To provide for the lease rental payments under the lease, the governing body must levy an annual tax sufficient to make such payments as they become due. The State Department of Local Government Finance is required to annually review the tax levy in a school corporation's debt service fund to determine whether such levy is sufficient to make the lease rental payments together with all other payments made out of the debt service fund. In addition, if a school corporation fails to pay any of the lease rental payments, the Treasurer of the State of Indiana is required to (a) intercept the money provided by the State of Indiana to the school corporation in an amount equal to the unpaid lease payment or payments which are due, and (b) forward the intercepted money to the trustee or lessor under the lease. This is known as the "State Intercept Mechanism," and it has been used on at least one occasion.

The school corporation may enter into a lease with the building corporation in anticipation of the purchase of a site and construction of a school building. However, the school corporation cannot make any lease rental payments under the lease until one or more of the buildings subject to the lease are able to be used and occupied by the school corporation. For this reason, projects involving the construction of new school buildings in the past required a portion of the first mortgage bond proceeds be set aside to be used to pay the interest on the first mortgage bonds until the completion of the new school building and the commencement of the lease rentals. Beginning in 1996, Indiana laws were changed allowing school corporations to lease existing school buildings during the construction of new school buildings. Once the new school building is completed, the existing school building transfers back to the school corporation and the new school building becomes subject to the lease. This allows for lease payments to begin much earlier in the repayment process and minimize or eliminate the use of first mortgage bond proceeds to pay interest on the first mortgage bonds.

E. Sale Process

1. General. Unlike the sale of general obligation bonds, first mortgage bonds may be sold by either a public sale or a negotiated sale. While federal and state agencies have conducted studies to determine which method of sale is more efficient and provides the lowest cost (including interest cost) to the issuer of the bonds, these studies are not conclusive. Issuers, who select the public sale method, usually do so because it avoids the decision on which company to use as the underwriter, and this decision can sometimes become a political issue for a school board. School corporations, which select the negotiated sale method, usually do so because it is a little less cumbersome process and allows the first mortgage bonds to be sold in a slightly shorter timeframe than the public sale method.

2. Public Sale. Under Indiana law the public sale method may be through the publication of either a notice of sale or a notice of intent to sell.

   (a) Notice of sale. The notice of sale method requires the notice to be published in at least two newspapers which are either published or circulated in the school corporation. This notice provides a general description of the terms of the first mortgage bonds such as the bond repayment schedule and the prepayment terms and the date and time by which each potential purchaser of the first mortgage bonds must submit a bid containing interest rates for each maturity of the first mortgage bonds and the purchase price to be paid by the potential purchaser. This notice must be published twice with at least one week between the first and second publication. In addition, the first publication must be at least fifteen days before the sale date, and the second publication must be at least three days before the sale date. On the date and time identified in the notice, the superintendent of the school corporation, the assistant superintendent for financial affairs of the school corporation, the business manager or the financial advisor for the school corporation, as the authorized representative of the building corporation, will receive all of the bids, tabulate the bids to determine which bidder is offering the lowest net interest cost on the first mortgage bonds, and then award the sale of the first mortgage bonds to the bidder who offered the lowest net interest cost on the first mortgage bonds. The net interest cost on the first mortgage bonds is determined by computing the total interest on all of the first mortgage bonds from the date of sale to the date of maturity and deducting from this amount the premium bid, if any, or adding to this amount any discount.

(b) Notice of Intent to Sell. The notice of intent to sell method requires the notice to be published in at least two newspapers which are either published or circulated in the school corporation. In addition, the notice must be published in a newspaper which circulates in Indianapolis. This notice provides a general description of the terms of the first mortgage bonds such as the bond repayment schedule and the prepayment terms and a statement that by a certain date and time identified in the notice any person interested in submitting a bid for the first mortgage bonds must provide in writing to the school corporation official or representative listed in the notice, as the authorized representative of the building corporation, the name, address, telephone number and facsimile number of the potential purchaser. This notice must be published twice with at least one week between the first and second publication. In addition, the second publication must be at least seven days prior to the deadline for potential purchasers to submit their written interest to bid on the first mortgage bonds. At least twenty-four hours prior to the sale of the first mortgage bonds, the school corporation's official or representative, as the authorized representative of the building corporation, will notify all the interested potential purchasers of the date and time by which all bids on the first mortgage bonds must be received by the school corporation's officer or representative. On the date and time identified in the twenty-four hour notice, the school corporation's official or representative will receive all of the bids, tabulate the bids to determine which bidder is offering the lowest net interest cost on the first mortgage bonds, and then award the sale of the first mortgage bonds to the bidder who offered the lowest net interest cost on the first mortgage bonds. The net interest cost on the first mortgage bonds is determined by computing the total interest on all of the first mortgage bonds from the date of sale to the date of maturity and deducting from this amount the premium bid, if any, or adding to this amount any discount.

3. Negotiated Sale. The negotiated sale method involves the school corporation, on behalf of the building corporation, hiring a company to purchase the first mortgage bonds. This company is known as an underwriter because it agrees to purchase the first mortgage bonds from the building corporation even if the company does not have people, banks, mutual funds, insurance companies or other entities committed to buy all of the first mortgage bonds. Therefore, the company is "underwriting" or guaranteeing the purchase of the first mortgage bonds. For this commitment, the underwriter is paid a fee, which is usually similar to the fee charged by the purchaser of the bonds in a public sale. At a date recommended by the underwriter based on activity in the tax-exempt bond market, the underwriter will provide fixed interest

rates on the first mortgage bonds and the purchase price of the first mortgage bonds, which interest rates, purchase price and underwriter's fee may be negotiated by the building corporation representative.

III. REQUIRED TERMS OF THE LEASE

A. Term

Under current Indiana law, the maximum term of the first mortgage bonds issued by a building corporation may not exceed twenty-five years. Because the term of the lease begins shortly before the beginning of the repayment term of the first mortgage bonds, the maximum term of any least may not be longer than twenty-six years.

B. Lease Options

All leases must provide the school corporation with the option to renew the lease upon similar terms and to purchase the property prior to the end of the term of the lease.

C. Triple Net Leases

Most of the standard leases require the school corporation, as the lessee, to pay for all property taxes, if any, utility bills, insurance premiums and maintenance associated with the building. In addition, most leases require the school corporation to maintain the property in good condition.

D. Termination

Upon the termination of the lease, the building corporation must return to the school corporation any money held by the corporation in excess of the amount needed to retire first mortgage bonds and to dissolve the lessor corporation. In addition, the property subject to the lease must be transferred from the building corporation to the school corporation.

IV. OPPOSITION METHODS AVAILABLE

A. Petition-Remonstrance Process

One way to challenge the execution of a lease is through the petition-remonstrance process. (Refer to "Petetion - Remonstrance Process" later in this Part II.)

B. Objection Process

Another way taxpayers can challenge the execution of a lease is through the objection process. Under Indiana law, following the execution of the lease, the school corporation must publish a notice of execution of the lease. This notice must be published only one time in one or two newspapers published or circulated in the boundaries of the school corporation. The objection process is triggered upon the occurrence of ten or more taxpayers, who own property in the school corporation, filing a petition in the office of the county auditor stating they object to the execution of the lease on the grounds that it is unnecessary or the lease rentals are unfair or unreasonable. The petition must be filed within thirty days after the notice of execution is published. When the taxpayers file the petition of objection, the county auditor will forward a certified copy of the petition and any other relevant information to the State Department of Local Government Finance. Within thirty days after receiving the objection petition, the State Department of Local Government Finance will hold a special hearing at a location in the school corporation, at which time objectors and supporters of the lease financing and the project present evidence and testimony to the representative or representatives of the State Department of Local Government Finance. Following this special hearing, the Commissioner of the State Department of Local Government Finance will issue an order which either denies or accepts the objection petition. An appeal of the order of the Commissioner of the State Department of Local Government Finance must be filed with the Indiana State Tax Court no later than thirty days after the order is issued.

C. Challenge of Validity

Finally, taxpayers can oppose the lease by challenging the validity of the lease in a court of law. An action to contest the validity of the lease must be brought within thirty days after the publication of the notice of execution of the lease. After the sale of the first mortgage bonds, an action to contest the validity of the first mortgage bonds must be brought within five days after the bond sale.

MISCELLANEOUS FINANCING METHODS

I. TAX ANTICIPATION WARRANTS

A. Purpose and Term Limitation

As discussed earlier, school corporations, like other local governmental units, receive most of their revenues twice a year in the form of property tax distributions. This money is usually received during the last few days of June and December. However, the expenses of each school corporation are incurred on a weekly, bi-weekly or monthly basis. This often creates cash flow deficits in one or more of a school corporation's funds until the property taxes are received in June and December. In order to eliminate these cash flow deficits, many school corporations issue tax anticipation warrants in an amount equal to or slightly larger than the anticipated cash flow deficit. These tax anticipation warrants are issued prior to the time such deficits occur, and the tax anticipation warrants are repaid no later than the end of the current year from the property taxes received by the school corporation in June and December.

B. Security

When a school corporation issues tax anticipation warrants, the school corporation must repay the principal of those warrants from only moneys on deposit in the fund into which the proceeds of the tax anticipation warrants are deposited. For example, a school corporation issues tax anticipation warrants and deposits the proceeds of the warrants into the school corporation's general fund to pay expenses identified in its general fund. At the end of the year when those tax anticipation warrants mature, the school corporation may only use money which is on deposit in its general fund to repay the principal of those tax anticipation warrants. However, the interest on the tax anticipation warrants may be repaid from either the fund into which the proceeds were deposited or from the school corporation's debt service fund.

C. Borrowing Limitations

1. State Law Limitation. Under Indiana law, the maximum principal amount of tax anticipation warrants which may be outstanding at anytime during the year to fund expenditures for the transportation fund, bus replacement fund, capital projects fund or the debt service fund must be 80% or less of the property tax collections anticipated to be received for such fund within the six months prior to the maturity of such tax anticipation warrants. Under Indiana law, the maximum principal amount of tax anticipation warrants which be outstanding at anytime during the year to fund expenditures for the general fund must be 80% or less of the property tax collections and state funds anticipated to be received for the general fund with the six months prior to the maturity of such tax anticipation warrants. This rule is found under Indiana Code 20-5-4, as amended. There is another Indiana law available to school corporations which limits the tax anticipation warrants to fifty percent of the

property tax collections received in a particular fund for the calendar year, but this is limited to school cities and school towns, and is not commonly used.

2.   Federal Tax Law Limitation. If the school corporation wants to issue the tax anticipation warrants with tax-exempt interest rates, the school corporation must show in a cash flow worksheet that unless the tax anticipation warrants are issued the anticipated cashflow deficit for a particular fund during the six months after the tax anticipation warrants are contemplated to be issued will be at least ninety percent of the principal amount of tax anticipation warrants to be issued for that particular fund. While the cash flow worksheet looks at the period which is six months after the tax anticipation warrants are issued, the cash flow worksheet should be prepared as if the tax anticipation warrants are not issued.

D. Sale Process

1.   All tax anticipation warrants must be sold through the public sale method unless they are sold to the Indiana Bond Bank, a local public improvement bond bank, the federal government or any agency of the federal government. While the notice of intent to sell method is available for the public sale of tax anticipation warrants, most school corporations use the notice of sale method because it is a slightly simpler method of sale. For a discussion of the notice of intent to sell method, see "General Obligation Bonds--Sale Process" earlier in this Part II.

2.   The notice of sale method requires the notice to be published in one or two newspapers which are either published or circulated in the school corporation. This notice provides a general description of the terms of the tax anticipation warrants such as the maturity schedule and the prepayment terms and the date and time by which each potential purchaser of the tax anticipation warrants must submit a bid containing interest rates for the tax anticipation warrants and the purchase price to be paid by the potential purchaser. This notice must be published twice with at least one week between the first and second publication. In addition, the first publication must be at least ten days before the sale date, and the second publication must be at least three days before the sale date. On the date and time identified in the notice, the superintendent of the school corporation, the assistant superintendent for financial affairs of the school corporation, the business manager or the financial advisor for the school corporation will receive all of the bids, tabulate the bids to determine which bidder is offering the lowest net interest cost on the tax anticipation warrants, and then recommend to the school board to award the sale of the tax anticipation warrants to the bidder who offered the lowest net interest cost on the tax anticipation warrants. The net interest cost on the tax anticipation warrants is determined by computing the total interest on all of the tax anticipation warrants from the date of sale to the date of maturity and deducting from this amount the premium bid, if any, or adding to this amount any discount.

MISCELLANEOUS FINANCING METHODS

II. SCHOOL BUS LOANS

A. Purpose and Term Limitation

Whenever a school corporation wishes to finance the purchase of one or more school buses, the school corporation may issue general obligation bonds or enter into a loan for such purpose. Any general obligation bonds or loans issued to finance the purchase of a school bus or buses must have a final maturity no later than six years after the issuance of the general obligation bonds or the loan.

B. Security

The payment of the principal and interest on all general obligation bonds are secured by property taxes levied and collected by the school corporation and deposited into the school corporation's debt service fund. The payment of the principal and interest on all loans for school buses are secured by property taxes levied and collected by the school corporation and deposited into the school corporation's debt service fund and may also be secured by a lien on the bus or buses purchased with the proceeds of the loan.

C. Debt Limitation

All loans and general obligation bonds issued to finance the purchase of a school bus or school buses are treated under Indiana law as indebtedness subject to the same debt limitations as all other general obligation bonds.

D. Approval Processes

All loans and general obligation bonds issued to finance the purchase of a school bus or school buses must comply with the same local and state approval processes as any general obligation bonds issued by the school corporation.

E. Sale Process

If the school corporation issues general obligation bonds to finance the purchase of a school bus or buses, the school corporation must follow the same public sale processes applicable to the sale of all other general obligation bonds. If the school corporation issues a loan to finance the purchase of a school bus or buses, the school corporation may negotiate for such loan on the terms and conditions acceptable to the school corporation and the lender, provided, however, the term of the loan may not exceed six years.

PART II: BORROWING

III. INSTALLMENT PAYMENT CONTRACTS FOR GUARANTEED ENERGY SAVINGS CONTRACTS

A. Purpose and Term Limitation

Whenever a school corporation wishes to finance the costs of a guaranteed energy savings contract under Indiana Code 36-1-12.5, as amended, the school corporation may enter into an installment payment contract with the qualified provider of the energy conservation measures. Under Indiana law, the term of an installment payment contract commences on the date of final installation of the energy conservation measure or measures and ends no later than the lesser of ten years thereafter or the average life of the energy conservation measure or measures installed.

B. Security

The principal and interest on installment payment contracts may be paid from either the school corporation's general fund or the school corporation's capital projects fund. The payments must be subject to the annual appropriation of the school corporation. Therefore installment payment contracts are not quite as highly rated (from a credit perspective) as general obligation bonds or building lease-financings.

C. Debt Limitation

Indiana law states that payments under installment payment contracts do not constitute indebtedness under the Indiana Constitution or laws. For this reason, the only limit on installment payment contracts is that which is determined by the school corporation based on the amount of money it has available to make payments on such contracts.

D. Approval Process

Installment payment contracts must be approved by only the school board as a part of the approval process for the guaranteed energy savings contract.

E. Sale Process

Installment payment contracts are usually sold pursuant to a negotiated sale in which the provider of the energy conservation measures assigns its rights to a bank or other financial institution selected by the school board. The selection by the school board of the bank or other financial institution may be done in any manner determined by the school board.

IV. COMMON SCHOOL FUND LOANS

A. Purpose and Term Limitation

Common school fund loans are loans provided by the State of Indiana to school corporations at rates which are often subsidized by the State of Indiana, and, therefore, are at an interest rate which is less than interest rates on bond or lease-financings. As dictated by the specific terms of the loan documents, school corporations may use the proceeds of common school fund loans for construction, renovation, expansion and equipping projects or for the purchase of technology equipment. Common school fund loans for the purchase of technology equipment are available to all school corporations in the State of Indiana. However, to qualify for a common school fund loan for construction, renovation, expansion and equipping projects, the applying school corporation (1) must be applying for the reconstruction of a building which was substantially damaged by fire or natural disaster, or (2) must be a school corporation which has an assessed valuation to pupil ratio within the lowest 40% of all school corporations in the State of Indiana. The proceeds of a common school fund loan for construction, renovation, expansion and equipping projects may not be used for such projects at facilities used or to be used primarily for interscholastic or extracurricular activities. The term of the common school fund loans for technology projects may be between two and five years from the completion of the technology project and for construction, renovation, expansion and equipping projects may not exceed five (5) years from the completion of the construction, renovation, expansion and equipping project.

B. Security

Because these loans are provided by the State of Indiana, a school corporation repays the principal and interest on these loans through a deduction of its State funds. The school corporation then includes such deductions in its annual debt service fund tax levy. Upon collection of the debt service fund tax levy, the school corporation transfers the amount of the deductions from the school corporation's debt service fund to its general fund.

C. Debt Limitation

Because these are loans provided by the State of Indiana, Indiana law does not treat these as indebtedness subject to any debt limitation.

D. Approval Process

1. 1028 Process--If a school corporation anticipates spending more than $1,000,000 in connection with a construction, renovation, expansion or equipping project, it must hold a public hearing on the project. This hearing is commonly referred to as the "1028 Public Hearing." (Refer to "Building Projects -- Public Construction" in Part I.)

PART II: BORROWING

2. Local Approval Process

(a) In all common school fund loans, there are four local approval steps which are usually taken by a school board in connection with the receipt of a common school fund loan. Those steps are: (i) the adoption of an authorization resolution; (ii) the convening of a public hearing on the appropriation of the proceeds of the bonds; (iii) the adoption of an additional appropriation resolution; and (iv) the completion of the common school fund loan application. The adoption of an authorization resolution is usually the first step taken in the approval process and if it is financing a project which is anticipated to cost more than $1,000,000, it is usually adopted at the conclusion of the 1028 Public Hearing. Sometime prior to the receipt of the common school fund loan, the school board must hold the additional appropriation public hearing. The notice for this hearing must be published at least ten days prior to the hearing. Following the hearing, the school board may adopt the additional appropriation resolution and instruct the treasurer of the school corporation to file a report of additional appropriation with the State Department of Local Government Finance. The final step in the local approval process is the completion of the common school fund loan application and filing it with the Indiana Department of Education.

(b) If the common school fund loan is financing a controlled project as defined under Indiana Code § 6-1.1-20, as amended, a school corporation must also go through all or a portion of the petition-remonstrance process. (Refer to "Petition - Remonstrance Process" later in this Part II.)

3. State Approval Process

Twice a year the State Board of Education reviews and awards common school fund loans to school corporations. Loans are awarded based on the amount of funds available to be loaned for each program. With respect to the loans for technology equipment, the amount of each loan will be on a pro rata basis among the applications received for that period. With respect to the loans for construction, renovation, expansion and equipping projects, loans will be received by the applicant school corporations based on each applicant's assessed value to pupil ratio relative to all of the other applicants and not on a pro rata basis; provided, however, a loan during each application period may only be for one school facility and is limited by a formula which multiplies the number of students able to attend the school facility by a specific dollar amount established by the State Board of Education.

E. Sale Process

Because the loans are issued by the State of Indiana, there is not any public or negotiated sale of common school fund loans. Instead, once the application is approved the school corporation submits invoices to the State of Indiana for payment as those invoices

MISCELLANEOUS FINANCING METHODS

are approved by the school board. Upon completion of the project, the school corporation notifies the State of Indiana of the completion of the project. At that time, the State of Indiana provides the school corporation with the repayment schedule for the loan.

V. EQUIPMENT LEASES

A. Purpose and Term Limitation

In lieu of purchasing equipment, a school corporation may enter into a lease for such equipment the terms and conditions of which are subject to negotiation between the school corporation and the successful bidder. All equipment leases must have a term of five years or less or be approved by the State Department of Local Government Finance.

B. Security

The lease rental payments under any equipment lease are usually payable from the school corporation's general fund, bus replacement fund or capital projects fund. In addition, the lease rental payments are subject to the annual appropriation of the school corporation. Therefore, installment payment contracts are not quite as highly rated (from a credit perspective) as general obligation bonds or building lease-financings.

C. Debt Limitation

As with building lease-financings, equipment lease-financings are not treated as indebtedness under Indiana law. Therefore, there is no limitation by the State of Indiana on the amount of lease-financings a school corporation may have outstanding from time to time.

D. Approval Process

The local approval process involves only the approval of the lease agreement by the school board. So long as the term of the lease is five years or less, no state approval of the equipment lease is required.

E. Sale Process

All leases are subject to public sale in the same manner as if the school corporation were purchasing the equipment.

THE PETITION-REMONSTRANCE PROCESS

I. GENERAL

A. Applicability

The petition-remonstrance laws generally apply to the issuance of any bond, as defined by the petition-remonstrance law, or the execution of any lease by a school corporation if the principal and interest on the bond or the lease rental payments under the lease are paid in whole or in part from the school corporation's debt service fund.

B. Exceptions

The petition-remonstrance laws do not apply to:

1. Tax anticipation warrants;

2. Obligations payable from any fund other than the school corporation's debt service fund;

3. Funding, refunding or judgment funding bonds;

4. Bonds or leases, the debt service or lease payments of which are payable from the school corporation's debt service fund but are reasonably anticipated by the school corporation to be paid from other funds or moneys received by the school corporation;

5. Bonds or leases which will finance a project which costs the school corporation $2,000,000 or less; or

6. Bonds or leases which will finance a project that is required by a court order holding that a federal law mandates the project.

C. Definitions

The petition-remonstrance laws have certain meanings for certain words or phrases, including the following:

1. "Bonds" means any bonds or other evidences of indebtedness, including general obligation bonds and common school funds, which are payable from the school corporation's debt service fund.

2. "Controlled project" means any project which is financed, in whole or in part, from bonds or leases subject to the petition-remonstrance laws.

3. "Lease" means any lease which is payable from the school corporation's debt service fund.

PART II: BORROWING

4.   "Project" means any project or purpose for which a school corporation may issue bonds or enter into a lease.

II.   THE PROCESS

A. Phase One--The Preliminary Determination Phase

1.   To begin the preliminary determination phase, the school board must hold a public hearing to provide information to the community regarding the project and the issuance of bonds or the execution of a lease to finance all or a portion of the project. The notice of this public hearing must be published at least ten days prior to the public hearing in one or two newspapers published or circulated in the school corporation's boundaries. In addition, this notice must be sent by first-class mail at least ten days prior to the public hearing to any organization which, prior to January 1 of that year, delivers a request to the school corporation to receive such notices.

2.   At the date and time identified in the public hearing notice, the school board will hold a public hearing to provide certain information to the community regarding the project and the bonds to be issued or the lease to be executed in order to finance all or a portion of the project. This preliminary determination public hearing is usually held simultaneously with the 1028 Public Hearing. (Refer to "Building Projects – Public Construction - Projects in Excess of $1,000,000" in Part I.) At the conclusion of the public hearing, the school corporation may adopt a resolution making a preliminary determination to issue bonds or enter into a lease. This resolution should include a general description of the project to be undertaken by the school corporation as well as the terms of the financing which are required to be in the notice of preliminary determination discussed in the paragraph 3 of this Section A. This resolution is only a preliminary determination by the school board, and it does not prevent the school board from rescinding this preliminary determination at any time during the legal process up until the bonds are issued or the lease executed by the school corporation.

3.   After the adoption of the preliminary determination resolution described in paragraph 2 of this Section A, the school corporation must publish the notice of this preliminary determination one time in one or two newspapers published or circulated in the boundaries of the school corporation. In addition, this notice must be sent by first-class mail to any organization which, prior to January 1 of that year, delivers a request to the school corporation to receive such notices. Under the petition-remonstrance laws, this notice must contain (a) a general description of the project to be financed with the bonds or the lease, (b) the maximum term of the bonds or the lease; (c) the maximum principal amount of the bonds or the maximum lease rental for the lease; because it is unclear under the laws, the notice should contain both the maximum annual lease rental and the maximum aggregate lease rental over the term of the lease; (d) the estimated interest rates and the total interest costs; and (e) a statement that any owners of real property within the school corporation

THE PETITION-REMONSTANCE PROCESS   69

who want to initiate a petition and remonstrance process against the financing must file a petition with the county auditor in compliance with Indiana Code 6-1.1-20-3.1(4) and (5) not later than thirty days after the preliminary determination notice is published. If the project being financed involves the construction of a new school facility or the renovation or expansion of an existing school facility, which has not be used for at least three years, the preliminary determination notice must also include the estimated costs the school corporation expects to incur annually to operate such facilities and a statement whether the school corporation expects to file a new facility appeal for the new facility.

B. Phase Two--The Request Phase

1. This phase begins immediately following the publication of the notice of preliminary determination described in paragraph 3 of Section A above, and lasts for thirty days after the publication of the notice of preliminary decision.

2. This phase provides the owners of real property within the boundaries of the school corporation to circulate a petition which requests the application of the petition-remonstrance process (phase three) to the proposed project and the financing. In order to trigger the petition-remonstrance process, the requesting petitions circulated by real property owners must be (a) signed by the lesser of one hundred owners of real property within the boundaries of the school corporation or five percent of the owners of real property within the boundaries of the school corporation, and (b) filed with the county auditor no later than thirty days after the publication of the notice of preliminary determination.

3. The requesting petitions must be (a) on the form created by the State Board of Accounts and provided to the county auditor, (b) accompanied by instructions detailing the signature, carrying and filing requirements of each petition, (c) carried by people who (i) are owners of real property within the geographical boundaries of the school corporation and (ii) have signed at least one of the requesting petitions, and (d) verified under oath by the carrier which is notarized by a notary public stating that the carrier witnessed each signature on that petition.

4. Within fifteen business days after receiving the petitions requesting the application of the petition-remonstrance process, the county auditor must provide the school board with a copy of the petitions and a certificate, which states the number of owners of real property within the geographical boundaries of the school corporation who signed the petition.

5. If a sufficient number of owners of real property within the geographical boundaries of the school corporation have filed valid petitions requesting the application of the petition-remonstrance process to the project or the financing within the thirty-day request period, then the school corporation must proceed to the third phase of the petition-remonstrance process described in Section C below or withdraw the project and the financing for at least one year. If valid petitions requesting the application

of the petition-remonstrance process to the project or the financing are not filed within the thirty-day request period or valid petitions are filed within the thirty-day request period but they do not contain signatures for a sufficient number of owners of real property within the geographical boundaries of the school corporation, then the school corporation is not required to proceed with any further phases of the petition-remonstrance process and needs to complete only the processes for issuing the bonds or executing the lease described in this Part II.

C. Phase Three--Petition-Remonstrance Carrying Process

1. Phase three begins with the publication by the school corporation of the notice of applicability of the petition-remonstrance carrying process to the project and the financing. This notice must be published one time in one or two newspapers published or circulated in the boundaries of the school corporation. In addition, this notice must be sent by first-class mail to any organization which, prior to January 1 of that year, delivers a request to the school corporation to receive such notices.

2. During this phase, the school corporation may not (a) allow any of the facilities or equipment of the school corporation to be used for public relations purposes to promote a position regarding the project or the financing unless equal access to such facilities or equipment is given to the people who have a position opposite to the school corporation's position, (b) make any expenditure of public funds to promote a position regarding the project or the financing (except as necessary to explain the project to the public) or to pay for the gathering of signatures, (c) use an employee to promote a position on the project or the financing during the employee's normal working hours or paid overtime, or (d) promote a position on the project or the financing by (i) using students to transport written materials to their residences or (ii) including a statement within another communication sent to the students' residences. These restrictions, however, do not prohibit an employee of the school corporation from carrying out duties with respect to this process which are part of the normal and regular conduct of the employee's office or agency.

3. During the first twenty-eight days after this notice of applicability is published the county auditor will prepare and print the petition forms which will be carried by owners of real property within the boundaries of the school corporation. The petition forms which state that the signers support the project and the financing are defined by the petition-remonstrance laws as the "petitions." The petition forms which state that the signers oppose the project and the financing are defined by the petition-remonstrance laws as the "remonstrances." These forms must be (a) on the forms created by the State Board of Accounts and provided to the county auditor, (b) accompanied by instructions detailing the signature, carrying and filing requirements of each petition, (c) carried by people who (i) are owners of real property within the geographical boundaries of the school corporation and (ii) have signed at least one of the petition or remonstrance counterparts, and (d) verified under oath by the carrier which is notarized by a notary public stating that the carrier witnessed each signature on that petition.

THE PETITION-REMONSTANCE PROCESS

4. On the twenty-ninth day after the notice of applicability is published, the petition and remonstrance counterparts can be obtained by owners of real property within the boundaries of the school corporation from the county auditor with the date of distribution written on each counterpart. A person may request one or more petition or remonstrance counterparts, and the person requesting such petition or remonstrance counterparts does not need to be the person who carries all of those counterparts. In fact, it is not uncommon for one or two people to be designated by the proponents and opponents of the project and the financing as the people responsible for obtaining all petition and remonstrance counterparts which will be distributed to their respective carriers.

5. Signed and verified petition and remonstrance counterparts must be filed with the county auditor no early than the thirtieth day (or the first business day thereafter if the thirtieth day falls on a weekend or a holiday) after the notice of applicability is published and no later than the sixtieth day (or the first business day thereafter if the sixtieth day falls on a weekend or a holiday) after the notice of applicability is published. During this carrying period, the petition-remonstrance laws prohibit anyone from soliciting or collecting signatures on property owned or controlled by the school corporation.

6. Within fifteen business days after receiving the petition or the remonstrance counterparts, the county auditor must file with the school board a copy of the filed petition or the remonstrance counterparts and a certificate, which states the number of people who (a) are real property owners in the boundaries of the school corporation and (b) signed either a petition counterpart or a remonstrance counterpart. Depending on the number of signatures on the petition and remonstrance counterparts, the county auditor's verification period may be extended up to a maximum of sixty days. If the number of real property owners on the valid remonstrance counterparts are greater than the number of real property owners on the valid petition counterparts, then the project is defeated, and the school corporation must repeat the first two phases of the petition-remonstrance process before proceeding with the financing of the project through the issuance of bonds or the execution of a lease. However, the school board may not make a preliminary determination to issue bonds or enter into a lease for the project or any other project that is not substantially different for one (1) year after it receives the county auditor's certificate regarding the number of signatures on the petition and remonstrance counterparts. If the number of real property owners on the valid petition counterparts are equal to or greater than the number of real property owners on the valid remonstrance counterparts, then the political subdivision may proceed with applicable lease or bond proceedings described in Part II of this Article I. If the school corporation is successful in the petition-remonstrance carrying phase, it is not required to follow any other remonstrance or objection procedures under any other law relating to the issuance of the bonds or the execution of the lease.

PART III

BUDGETING

BUDGETS, APPROPRIATIONS & PUBLIC FUND LAWS • THE PRIMARY FUNDS OF A SCHOOL CORPORATION • GENERAL FUND REFERENDUM PROCESS

BUDGETS, APPROPRIATIONS AND PUBLIC FUND LAWS

I. THE BUDGET PROCESS

A. Establishment of the True Tax Value

On December 4, 1998, the Indiana Supreme Court affirmed a ruling by the Indiana Tax Court that the property wealth assessment methodology employed in the 1995 Indiana Real Property Assessment Manual was unconstitutional. <u>State Bd. of Tax Comm'rs v. Town of St. John</u>, 702 N.E.2d 1034 (Ind. 1998). The Indiana Supreme Court ruled that the reproduction cost schedules used by the State Board of Tax Commissioners (the "State Board") were arbitrary and unconstitutional. As a result, the State Board issued new regulations, a manual, and guidelines in May 2001 (the "Regulations") to comply with the Supreme Court's decision. The Regulations were effective as of the March 1, 2002 assessment date and affect the property taxes payable in 2003. The Regulations shifted the tax burden among various classes of property owners, but were not intended to impact the total tax levy. This ruling affected only the valuation method and not the ability of school corporations and other local governmental units to levy property taxes.

As of January 1, 2002, the State legislature dissolved the State Board and created two new agencies to replace the State Board, the Indiana Department of Local Government Finance ("DLGF") and the Indiana Board of Tax Review (the "IBTR"). The DLGF assumed the administrative responsibilities of the State Board and the IBTR assumed the responsibilities of the State Board for property tax appeals.

Real and personal property in the State of Indiana is assessed each year as of March 1st. On or before August 1st each year, each county auditor must submit to certain local, county, and state agencies a statement providing (1) information concerning the assessed valuation in the school corporation for the next calendar year, (2) an estimate of the taxes to be distributed to the school corporation during the last six months of the current calendar year, (3) the current assessed valuation as shown on the abstract of charges, (4) the average growth in assessed valuation in the school corporation over the preceding three budget years, excluding years in which a general reassessment occurs, and (5) any other relevant information.

Historically, real property was assessed at its depreciated reproduction cost, whereas personal property was assessed at historical cost less depreciation. Under the Regulations, real property is now assessed at its market value in use. Personal property continues to be assessed at historical cost less depreciation. Inventory generally is assessed at its historical cost less certain other adjustments. There are certain credits, deductions and exemptions available for various classes of property. For instance, residential real property is eligible for certain deductions for mortgages, veterans, the aged and the blind. Commercial and industrial real property, new manufacturing equipment and research and development equipment may be entitled to economic revitalization area deductions. Business inventories may be eligible for enterprise zone credits. Government-owned properties and properties owned, used and occupied for charitable, literary, scientific, educational or religious purposes may be entitled to exemptions from tax. The gross assessed value less all such deductions, credits and exemptions (the "True Tax Value") is the value used for taxing purposes in the determination of tax rates.

Assessed values of real property change periodically as a result of general reassessments scheduled by the State legislature, as well as when changes occur in the property due to new construction or demolition of improvements. The last general reassessment of property in the State is effective for taxes assessed March 1, 2002, for taxes payable in 2003. The next reassessment is scheduled to begin July 1, 2007, and is scheduled to take effect for 2009 pay 2010. Reassessments are scheduled to occur every four years thereafter.

When a change in assessed value occurs, a written notification is sent to the affected property owner. If the owner wishes to appeal this action with respect to an assessment date prior to March 1, 2004, the owner may file a request for preliminary conference with the township assessor of the township in which the property is located within 45 days after (1) a notice of a change in assessment is given to the taxpayer, or (2) the taxpayer receives a tax statement for the property taxes that are based on the assessment for the assessment date, whichever occurs first. Beginning with the March 1, 2005 assessment date, an owner may appeal the assessed value of his or her property at any time, regardless of whether a change in the assessed value has been made. Those appeals generally may be filed no later than May 10 of each year the owner wishes to appeal. An appeal filed after May 10 is effective for the following year's assessment.

Appeal petitions are reviewed by the county property tax assessment board of appeals in the county where the property is located. If the owner does not receive a favorable ruling from the county board, the owner may file a petition for review to the IBTR. If the owner does not receive a favorable ruling from the IBTR, the owner may file a petition with the Indiana Tax Court. In addition, local officials may also appeal decisions of the IBTR to the Tax Court. While an appeal is pending and unless collection of the tax is stayed, any taxes on real property which become due must be paid in an amount based on the immediately preceding year's assessment. Any taxes on personal property which become due while the property is subject to appeal must be paid based on the assessed value reported on the personal property tax return.

B. Establishment of the Budget

Under Indiana law, the budget, tax levy, tax rates and appropriations of each school corporation (other than the South Bend Community School Corporation, which would be no later than its respective last meeting in September) must be established no later than September 20 of each year. At least ten days prior to the adoption of the annual budget, the school board must hold a public hearing on the budget. The notice for this public hearing must be published in one or two newspapers which are published or generally circulated in the geographical boundaries of the school corporation. The notice must be published one time at least ten days prior to the public hearing; provided, however, if a notice of the public

BUDGETS, APPROPRIATIONS & PUBLIC FUND LAW

hearing fails to be published at least ten days prior to the public hearing as a result of error by the newspaper, the notice will be deemed under Indiana law to satisfy the publication requirements of the statute as long as it is published at least three days prior to the public hearing. The notice of the public hearing must contain the estimated budget, the maximum permissible levy, the current and proposed tax levies of each fund, the amounts of excessive levy appeals to be requested and the date, time and place of the public hearing on the budget. If there is an error in the numbers in the notice which is due to the fault of the newspaper, the notice is still considered a valid notice under Indiana law.

Once adopted by the school board, the budget, tax levies, tax rates and appropriations are subject to review and revision by the county board of tax adjustment governing the school corporation, which can lower, but not raise the tax levy or tax rate. Taxpayers of the school corporation may challenge the budget, tax levy and tax rate approved by the school board. In addition, taxpayers of the school corporation or the school corporation may initiate an appeal of the budget and tax levies approved by the county board of tax adjustment to the DLGF. The DLGF may revise or reduce the budget, tax levies, tax rates and appropriations, or may increase the budget, tax levies, tax rates and appropriations, but such increases generally may not exceed the amount originally approved by the school board, except under certain limited circumstances.

On or before March 15 of the immediately following year, the county auditor is required to prepare and deliver to the Indiana State Auditor and county treasurer the final abstract of the property, assessments, taxes, deductions, and exemptions for taxes payable in that year in each taxing district within that county, including the school corporation. The county treasurer generally mails tax statements in April of that year (but mailing may be delayed due to reassessment and other factors). Property taxes are due and payable to the county treasurer in two installments on May 10th and November 10th. If an installment of taxes is not completely paid on or before the due date, a penalty of 10% of the delinquent amount is added to the amount due. If the delinquent amount is not paid, real property generally becomes subject to tax sale after July 1 in the year after the tax was due. With respect to delinquent personal property taxes, the county treasurer in which the property is located may initiate collection procedures after November 10 in the year the tax was due.

C. Fund Accounting

The Indiana State Board of Accounts regulations require a ledger account on a specific form created by the Indiana State Board of Accounts must be created and used for each fund created by a school corporation. The ledger account will record all receipts and disbursements for that fund which occur during the year. In addition, an aggregate ledger account for all funds must be maintained by each school corporation. The Indiana State Board of Accounts has set forth specific guidelines in its accounting manuals for the posting of receipts and disbursements from each ledger account.

II. APPROPRIATIONS

A. General

Under Indiana law, appropriations must be established for each expenditure from any fund of a school corporation. An appropriation is merely a pre-approval to spend an identified amount of money for a specific purpose. Appropriations are allocated in the form of amounts for certain programs within specific funds of the school corporation. Expenditures for each program within a particular fund are limited to such appropriation amounts unless additional appropriations are made. All appropriations, except appropriations of money from the capital projects fund and proceeds of bonds, notes or other obligations issued by a school corporation, quasi-public corporation or any authorized body of the school corporation expire at the end of the current budget year. Appropriations from the capital projects fund or proceeds of bonds, notes or other obligations issued by a school corporation, quasi-public corporation or any authorized body of the school corporation for a specific project remain in full force and effect until the purpose for which the appropriation was made has been accomplished or abandoned.

B. Additional Appropriations

If the school board determines that an expenditure either is not included within a current available program appropriation or is in excess of the current available program appropriations, the school board must approve an additional appropriation in the amount of such expenditure. Prior to approving such additional appropriation, the school board must hold a public hearing on the additional appropriation. The notice of the public hearing must be published in one or two newspapers generally circulated or published in the geographical boundaries of the school corporation. The notice must be published one time at least ten days prior to the public hearing. If the additional appropriation is in a fund which receives property tax collections, the additional appropriation must be approved by both the school board and the Indiana Department of Local Government Finance. If the additional appropriation is in a fund which does not receive any property tax collections, then the additional appropriation must be approved by only the school board, but a report of the additional appropriation must be filed with the Indiana Department of Local Government Finance.

III. FUND TRANSFERS

Under Indiana law there are two types of transfers. One type of transfer involves the transfer of money from one major budget classification to another budget classification within the same fund. Any transfers of this type may only be done if the school board determines (A) such transfer is necessary, (B) the transfer does not require the expenditure of more money than the total amount set out in the budget, and (C) the transfer is approved at a regular meeting of the school board. No repayment of these transfers within a fund are required. These transfers within a fund may be done without notice to or approval of the Indiana Department of Local Government Finance. The other type of transfers involves the transfer of money from one fund to another fund. To make any such transfers (A) the fund

BUDGETS, APPROPRIATIONS & PUBLIC FUND LAW

receiving the transfer must be in need of money for cashflow purposes, (B) the fund from which the money is being transferred must contain sufficient money on deposit to provide for such transfer, (C) except in certain circumstances discussed below in this paragraph, the amount transferred must be returned to the original fund by the end of the budget year of the year in which the transfer is made, and (D) the transfers must be from only revenues derived from the levying and collecting of property taxes or special taxes or from the operations of the school corporation. While Indiana law requires such transfers to be repaid by the end of the current budget year, Indiana law does allow the school board to extend the repayment period for up to six months into the next budget year if the school board by resolution (A) determines an emergency exists that requires an extension of the repayment to a date which is no later than six months after the end of the current budget year (B) provides a brief description of the grounds for the emergency, and (C) identifies the date the transfer will be repaid. Any such resolution adopted by the school board must be immediately forwarded to the Indiana State Board of Accounts and the Indiana Department of Local Government Finance.

IV. DEPOSIT AND INVESTMENT OF PUBLIC FUNDS

A. Definitions

1.   Indiana law defines a depository as a financial institution designated as a depository of public funds.

2.   Indiana law defines a financial institution as (a) a bank, trust company or mutual savings bank which (i) is incorporated under Indiana law or the law of any other state, and (ii) has its principal office or a branch in Indiana, (b) a national banking association with its principal office or a branch in Indiana, (c) a savings association operating as a deposit association incorporated under Indiana law, (d) a federally chartered savings association with its principal office or branch in Indiana, (e) a federally chartered savings bank with its principal office or a branch in Indiana, or (f) a state chartered credit union in Indiana which (i) is federally insured or privately insured and (ii) has assets of at least $3,000,000.

B. Deposit of Public Funds

1.   Under Indiana law, a school corporation may deposit its funds in any financial institution which (a) is a depository eligible to receive state funds, and (b) unless an exception described in clause 2 applies, has a principal office or branch located within the geographical boundaries of the school corporation which is willing to accept public funds.

2.   In some instances, there are school corporations which do not have a financial institution which meets the requirements set forth in clause 1 or only have one financial institution which meet the requirements set forth in clause 1. If a school corporation does not have a financial institution which meets the requirements set forth in clause, then the school board may designate one or more financial institutions,

which are located outside the geographical boundaries of the school corporation, to serve as the depository or depositories of the school corporation. If a school corporation has only one financial institution which meets the requirements set forth in clause 1, then the school board may treat that qualifying financial institution as if it were not located inside the geographical boundaries of the school corporation and designate one or more financial institutions, which are located outside the geographical boundaries of the school corporation including the qualifying financial institution now designated to be outside the school corporation's boundaries, to serve as the depository or depositories of the school corporation.

3.   If more there is more than one qualifying financial institution available to the school corporation, the school corporation may have to maintain deposits with more than one of the qualifying financial institutions. If the monthly average balance on deposit in the accounts is $100,000 or less, then the school corporation may maintain all of its deposits at one qualifying financial institution. If the monthly average balance on deposit in the accounts exceeds $100,000, then the school corporation must maintain deposit accounts in at least two of the qualifying financial institutions, but the amount of the deposits does not have to be equal among such financial institutions.

C. Investment of Public Funds

1.   In general, a school corporation may invest in (a) securities backed by the full faith and credit of the United States Treasury or fully guaranteed by the United States and issued by (i) the United States Treasury, (ii) a federal agency, (iii) a federal instrumentality, or (iv) a federal government sponsored enterprise, (b) securities fully guaranteed and issued by (i) a federal agency, (ii) a federal instrumentality, or (iii) a federal government sponsored enterprise, (c) money market mutual funds that are in the form of securities of or interests in an open-end, no-load, management-type investment company or investment trust registered under the provisions of the federal Investment Company Act of 1940, as amended, (d) repurchase agreements or (e) certificates of deposits.

2.   Investments must have a stated maturity of two years or less.

3.   Investments in money market mutual funds and repurchase agreements must be with only financial institutions which qualify for deposits of the school corporation under Section B above.

4.   Investments in money market mutual funds may not exceed fifty percent of the funds held by the school corporation which are available for investment. The portfolio of the investment company or investment trust must be limited to (a) direct obligations of the United States, (b) obligations issued by (i) a federal agency, (ii) a federal instrumentality, or (iii) a federal government sponsored enterprise, and (c) repurchase agreements fully collateralized by the obligations described in clauses (a) or (b) of this paragraph 4. The form of securities of or interests in an investment

BUDGETS, APPROPRIATIONS & PUBLIC FUND LAW

company or investment trust must be rated (a) AAAm, or its equivalent, by Standard & Poor's Ratings Services or its successor, or (b) Aaa, or its equivalent, by Moody's Investors Service, Inc. or its successor. Money market mutual funds are deemed by Indiana law to have a stated final maturity of one day.

5. Investments in repurchase agreements must be fully collateralized by interest-bearing obligations which are issued, fully insured or fully guaranteed by (a) the United States, (b) a United States government agency, (c) an instrumentality of the United States, or (d) a federal government sponsored enterprise. Repurchase agreements are deemed by Indiana law to have a stated final maturity of one day.

6. Investments in certificates of deposit must be authorized by a resolution of the school board which is not more than two years old. In order to invest in certificates of deposit, the school corporation must solicit quotes for certificates of deposit from at least three depositories, including at least one or two depositories which qualify for deposits of the school corporation under Section B above. The quotes may be either in writing or on the phone, and a memorandum of all quotes solicited and taken will be retained by the school corporation as a public record. Investments in certificates of deposit must be placed in the depository quoting the highest rate of interest, after deducting any fee charged by the depository. If two or more depositories provide the same highest quote, the investing officer of the school corporation may select which depository will receive the investment. However, if only one of the two or more depositories providing the same highest quote is a depository which qualifies for deposits of the school corporation under Section B above, then the investing officer of the school corporation must invest the money with such depository.

7. Interest on all investments may be deposited into any fund of the school corporation pursuant to a resolution adopted by the school board regarding the deposit of such interest, including the school corporation's general fund, unless interest must be receipted to a specific fund as required by federal law or regulation or court order.

8. Any officer of the school corporation who knowingly violates or fails to perform any duty imposed by the Indiana public fund laws commits at least a Class B misdemeanor.

THE PRIMARY FUNDS OF A SCHOOL CORPORATION

I. GENERAL DISCUSSION

In all school corporations there are six basic funds into which property taxes and other revenues of the school corporation are deposited. Those six basic funds are the general fund, the transportation fund, the bus replacement fund, the capital projects fund, the debt service fund and the special education pre-school fund. In addition to these six basic funds, many school corporations have established a rainy day fund, a retirement/severance bond fund, a retirement/severance bond debt service fund, a post-retirement/severance future benefits fund, a construction fund, a school lunch fund and a textbook rental fund. While some of these funds receive property tax money, several of these funds are funded from several different sources such as bond proceeds, federal and state grants or student fees. In addition, there are other miscellaneous funds established by school corporations from time to time, and the State Board of Accounts' compliance manual identifies most all of those miscellaneous funds and the corresponding accounting number to be used by the school corporation when such funds are established. Because many of these miscellaneous funds are used on only an infrequent and somewhat uncommon basis, we will not spend anytime in this section discussing these miscellaneous funds.

A. General Fund

A school corporation's general fund is established and operated under Indiana Code 21-2-11, as amended, and is designated by the State Board of Accounts and the State Department of Local Government Finance as Fund No. 010. Money deposited into the general fund may be used by the school corporation to pay any expense of the school corporation, including, but not limited to debt service payments, lease payments and payments for building projects and maintenance. However, money deposited into the general fund may not be used to pay for student transportation costs. The general fund is known as a "levy limited fund," which means the amount of annual property tax dollars which may be levied and collected for deposit into a school corporation's general fund is limited based on the school corporation's general fund for the prior year and then calculated using a formula established under Indiana law. Every expenditure out of the general fund must be included within an appropriation approved by the State Department of Local Government Finance.

B. Transportation Fund

A school corporation's transportation fund is established and operated under Indiana Code 21-2-11.5, as amended, and is designated by the State Board of Accounts and the State Department of Local Government Finance as Fund No. 041. Money deposited into the transportation fund may be used by the school corporation to pay for all of the operating costs attributable to the transportation of the school corporation's students, including (A) the salaries paid to all bus drivers, transportation supervisors, mechanics and garage employees, clerks and other transportation-related employees (such employees do not include teaching personnel or principals, but do include instructional aids who are assigned to assist with the school transportation program, (B) contracted transportation service other than costs payable from the bus replacement fund, (C) wages of independent contractors, (D) payments to common carriers under contract, (D) student fares, (E) transportation related insurance premiums, and (F) other expenses of operating the school corporation's transportation service, including gasoline, lubricants, tires, repairs, contracted repairs, parts, supplies equipment and other related expenses. The transportation fund is a levy limited fund based on a formula prescribed by Indiana law. Every expenditure out of the transportation fund must be included within an appropriation approved by the State Department of Local Government Finance.

In extreme situations, a school corporation may be able to obtain an increase in its property tax levy above the levy allowed by the formula. To obtain this special increase, the school corporation must establish that (A) the school corporation will not be able to provide transportation services without the increase, and (B) the increase is necessary due to a transportation cost increase of at least ten percent over the preceding year as a result of (1) an increase in fuel costs, (2) a significant increase in the number of students enrolled in the school corporation that need transportation, (3) a significant increase in the mileage traveled by the school corporation's buses compared to the previous year, (4) a significant increase in the number of students enrolled in special education who need transportation, (5) a significant increase in the mileage traveled by the school corporation's buses due to students enrolled in special education as compared to the previous year, (6) increased transportation operating costs due to compliance with a court ordered desegregation plan, or (7) the closure of a school building with the school corporation that results in a significant increase in the distances that students must be transported to attend another school building.

C. Bus Replacement Fund

A school corporation's bus replacement fund is established and operated under Indiana Code 21-2-11.5, as amended, and is designated by the State Board of Accounts and the State Department of Local Government Finance as Fund No. 042. Money deposited into the bus replacement fund may be used by the school corporation to pay for (A) the purchase of all school buses, either through purchase agreements or lease agreements, or (B) all or a portion of the cost of contracted service, if such cost is designated by the school board in the year prior to the first school year in which the contract commences.

The bus replacement fund's levy and tax rate are not limited by any formula under Indiana law. However, to be able to levy a property tax for the bus replacement fund, a school board must hold a public hearing on a school bus replacement plan, adopt a resolution approving the school bus replacement plan, and receive approval of the school bus replacement plan from the State Department of Local Government Finance. The format of a school corporation's school bus replacement plan must (A) be in the format prescribed by the State Department of Local Government Finance, (B) be for a term of at least ten budget years immediately following the year the plan is adopted, (C) include (1) an estimate for each year of the plan the nature and amount of the proposed expenditures from the bus replacement fund, (2) a presumption that the minimum useful life of a school bus is not less than ten years, (3) the source of all revenue to be used to pay such expenditures in each budget year, (4) the amount of property taxes to be collected in each year, and (5) the cash balance to be retained

THE PRIMARY FUNDS OF A SCHOOL CORPORATION

in the bus replacement fund for expenditures in later years. If a school bus replacement plan includes the acquisition of additional school buses or school buses which contain a larger seating capacity than the number or type of school buses purchased in the prior year, the school bus replacement plan must contain evidence supporting the demand for increased transportation services in the school corporation. If a school bus replacement plan includes the replacement of a school bus earlier than ten years after the school bus was purchased, the school bus replacement plan must contain evidence supporting the need for such early replacement. A school corporation may amend its school bus replacement plan at any time, but such amendment must be the subject of a public hearing, must be approved by the school board and must be approved by the State Department of Local Government Finance.

D. Debt Service Fund

A school corporation's debt service fund is established and operated under Indiana Code 21-2-4, as amended, and is designated by the State Board of Accounts and the State Department of Local Government Finance as Fund No. 020. Money deposited into the debt service fund may be used by the school corporation to pay for (A) the debt service on all debt and other obligations arising out of funds borrowed or advanced for school buildings; (B) the lease payments on all leases to provide capital construction; (C) the interest on all emergency and temporary loans; (D) the debt service on all debt and other obligations arising out of funds borrowed or advanced for the purchase or lease of school buses when purchased or leased from the proceeds of a bond issue, or from money obtained from a loan under IC § 20-9.1-6-5, for that purpose; (E) the debt service on all debt and other obligations arising out of funds borrowed to pay judgments against the school corporation; or (F) the debt service on all debt and other obligations arising out of funds borrowed to purchase equipment. Prior to the commencement of making any payments out of the debt service fund for the obligations listed in clauses (A), (B), (D), (E) or (F), incurring such obligations or executing such leases must be approved by the State Department of Local Government Finance.

The debt service fund levy and tax rate are not limited, and the school board is required by law to establish a tax levy each year which is sufficient to pay all of the debt service payments, interest payments and lease payments set forth above. If the State Department of Local Government Finance determines the debt service fund levy advertised by the school corporation is not sufficient to pay all of the annual debt service, lease and interest payments of the school corporation for a particular year, then the State Department of Local Government Finance may increase the debt service fund levy to an amount which is sufficient to make such payments. Every expenditure out of the debt service fund must be included within an appropriation approved by the State Department of Local Government Finance.

E. Capital Projects Fund

A school corporation's capital projects fund is established and operated under Indiana Code 21-2-15, as amended, and is designated by the State Board of Accounts and the State Department of Local Government Finance as Fund No. 035. Money deposited into the capital projects fund may be used by the school corporation to pay (A) with respect to any facility used or to be used by the school corporation (other than a facility used or to be used primarily for interscholastic or extracurricular activities) the costs of (1) planned construction, repair, replacement, or remodeling of such facilities; (2) site acquisition in connection with a facility or facilities; (3) site development in connection with a facility or facilities; or (4) repair, replacement, or site acquisition in connection with a facility or facilities that is necessitated by an emergency; (B) the costs of purchasing, leasing, repairing, or maintaining equipment to be used by the school corporation (other than vehicles to be used for any purpose and equipment to be used primarily for interscholastic or extracurricular activities); (C) the costs of purchasing, leasing, upgrading, maintaining, or repairing computer hardware and/or computer software, or computer hardware and software; (D) for the services of full-time or part-time computer maintenance employees; (E) the costs of nonrecurring in-service technology training of school employees; (F) advances, together with interest on the advances, from the common school fund for educational technology programs; (G) the costs of acquiring any equipment or services necessary (1) to implement a technology preparation curriculum, (2) to participate in a program to provide educational technologies, including computers, in the homes of students (commonly referred to as "the buddy system project", the 4R's technology program or any other program under the educational technology program established by Indiana law, (3) or to obtain any combination of such equipment or services; (H) the cost of acquisition by vocational building trade classes of (1) building sites, (2) buildings in need of renovation (3) building materials and equipment for the purpose of constructing new buildings and/or remodeling existing buildings; (I) lease payments under leases of real property, not including leases entered under Indiana Code 21-5-9 through Indiana Code 21-5-12, as amended; (J) for services of school corporation employees, who are brick layers, stone masons, cement masons, tile setters, glaziers, insulation workers, asbestos removers, painters, paperhangers, drywall applicators and tapers, plasterers, pipe fitters, roofers, structural and steel workers, metal building assemblers, heating and air conditioning installers, welders, carpenters, electricians, or plumbers as these occupations are defined in the U.S. Department of Labor, Employment and Training Administration, Dictionary of Occupational Titles, Fourth Edition, Revised 1991 if (1) the employees perform construction of, renovation of, remodeling of, repair of, or maintenance on the facilities and equipment specified in clauses (A) or (B) above, (2) the school corporation's total annual salary and benefits paid by the school corporation to employees described are at least six hundred thousand dollars, and (3) the payment of the employees described is included as part of the school corporation's capital projects fund plan; (K) for energy savings or installment payment contracts; (L) the construction, repair, replacement, remodeling or maintenance of school sports facilities as long as the annual amount paid from the capital projects fund for these purposes does not exceed five percent of the property tax revenues levied for the capital projects fund in that calendar year. In the last couple of years, the General Assembly has also authorized a certain amount of the school corporation's insurance premiums and utility expenses to be paid from its capital projects fund. However, this authorization is subject to a renewal by the General Assembly every year or two. Every expenditure out of the capital projects fund must be included within an appropriation approved by the State Department of Local Government Finance.

The capital projects fund levy and tax rate are limited based on the tax rate for the capital projects fund, which is adjusted each year based on a statutory formula taking into

THE PRIMARY FUNDS OF A SCHOOL CORPORATION 87

account the changes in the true tax value of the school corporation. However, to levy for the capital projects fund, a school board must establish a capital projects plan. The capital projects plan must (A) cover at least three years after the year the plan is adopted, (B) be in the format prescribed by the State Department of Local Government Finance, and (C) estimate (1) for each year the nature and amount of proposed expenditures from the capital projects fund, (2) the source of all revenue to be dedicated to the proposed expenditures, and (3) the amount of property taxes to be collected in each year and retained in the capital projects fund for expenditures proposed for a later year.

To establish a capital projects plan, a school board must hold a public hearing on a capital projects plan, prior to September 20 of the current year adopt a resolution approving the capital projects plan, and publish in one or two newspapers published or generally circulated in the geographical boundaries of the school corporation a notice of adoption of the resolution approving the capital projects plan. The notice of the adoption of the capital projects plan must be published no later than twenty days after the county auditor posts and publishes the notice of the school corporation's tax rate for the immediately following year. The publication of this notice triggers a ten-day period during which at least ten taxpayers may file a petition with the county auditor objecting to the proposed capital projects plan. If such a petition with a sufficient number of valid taxpayer signatures is not filed, then the capital projects fund is established in the immediately following year. If such a petition with a sufficient number of valid taxpayer signatures is filed, then the county auditor forwards the objecting petition to the State Department of Local Government Finance. After receiving notice of this objecting petition, the State Department of Local Government Finance will (A) establish a public hearing to be held in a location within the county in which the school corporation is located and (B) notify the school board and the first ten taxpayers on the objecting petition of the date, time and location of the public hearing. Following the hearing, the State Department of Local Government Finance will either approve, disapprove or modify the capital projects plan. This decision by the State Department of Local Government Finance may be appealed for up to forty-five days after such decision. Any amendment to a school corporation's capital project plan must comply with the same procedures, except the resolution approving the amendment to the capital projects plan may be adopted after September 20 of the current year, and such amendment must be submitted to the State Department of Local Government Finance for approval even if a valid objecting petition is not filed during the ten-day objecting period.

F. Special Education Preschool Fund

A school corporation's special education preschool fund is established and operated under Indiana Code 21-2-17, as amended, and is designated by the State Board of Accounts and the State Department of Local Government Finance as Fund No. 060. Money deposited into the special education preschool fund may be used by the school corporation to pay for all of the costs attributable to special education programs for preschool age children. The special education preschool fund levy and tax rate are limited to thirty-three hundredths of one cent per one hundred dollars of true tax value. Every expenditure out of the special education preschool fund must be included within an appropriation approved by the State Department of Local Government Finance.

G. Rainy Day Fund

A school corporation may establish and operate a rainy day fund pursuant to Indiana Code §36-1-8-5.1, as amended, and if such a fund is established it is designated by the State Board of Accounts and the State Department of Local Government Finance as Fund No. 061. To establish and operate a rainy day fund, the school board must adopt a resolution (A) establishing a rainy day fund, (B) identifying the purposes of the rainy day fund, and (C) identifying the sources of funding of the rainy day fund. In any fiscal year, a school corporation may transfer to the rainy day fund any unused and unencumbered money from the other funds of the school corporation, provided all such transfers must occur after the last day of the school corporation's fiscal year and before March 1 of the immediately following year and the aggregate amount of such transfers do not exceed ten percent of the school corporation's total annual budget for such year. Money deposited into the rainy day fund may be used by the school corporation to pay for any costs permitted by the resolution establishing the rainy day fund. There is no levy or tax rate permitted for the rainy day fund, and the State Department of Local Government Finance may not require the use of money in the rainy day fund to reduce the actual or maximum permissible levy of any other fund of the school corporation. Every expenditure out of the rainy day fund must be included within an appropriation approved by the State Department of Local Government Finance.

H. Retirement/Severance Bond Fund

A school corporation may establish and operate a retirement/severance bond fund pursuant to Indiana Code §20-5-4-1.7, as amended, and if such a fund is established it is designated by the State Board of Accounts and the State Department of Local Government Finance as Fund No. 062. A retirement/severance bond fund is established by a school corporation whenever the school corporation issues general obligation pension bonds. The school corporation deposits the proceeds of the general obligation pension bonds into the retirement/severance bond fund and uses the money deposited into the retirement/severance bond fund to pay the retirement benefits of the employees either through a one-time buy-out or through payments to the employees as each employee retires. There is no levy or tax rate permitted for the retirement/severance bond fund. Every expenditure out of the retirement/severance bond fund must be included within an appropriation approved by the State Department of Local Government Finance.

I. Retirement/Severance Bond Debt Service Fund

A school corporation may establish and operate a retirement/severance bond debt service fund pursuant to Indiana Code §20-5-4-1.7, as amended, and if such a fund is established it is designated by the State Board of Accounts and the State Department of Local Government Finance as Fund No. 025. A retirement/severance bond debt service fund is established by a school corporation whenever the school corporation issues general obligation pension bonds, and is used to pay the principal of and interest on the general obligation pension bonds as such principal and interest is due. Prior to issuing any general obligation pension bonds, the State Department of Local Government Finance must approve the issuance of such bonds. The retirement/severance bond debt service fund levy and tax

THE PRIMARY FUNDS OF A SCHOOL CORPORATION

rate are not limited, and the school board is required by law to establish a tax levy each year which is sufficient to pay all of the principal and interest of the general obligation pension bonds which is due in such year. However, the amount of the levy for a school corporation's retirement/severance bond debt service fund must be offset by an equal levy reduction in a school corporation's capital projects fund, bus replacement fund, transportation fund or any combination of any such funds. Every expenditure out of the debt service fund must be included within an appropriation approved by the State Department of Local Government Finance.

J. Post-Retirement/Severance Future Benefits Fund

A school corporation must establish and operate a post-retirement/severance future benefits fund pursuant to Indiana Code 20-5-64, as amended, whenever (A) a school corporation establishes a retirement or severance plan after June 30, 2001, which requires the school corporation to pay post-retirement or severance benefits to employees of the school corporation, or (B) a school corporation includes in a collective bargaining agreement or other contract entered into by the school corporation after June 30, 2001, the provisions of which (1) increase the post-retirement or severance benefits, or (2) the unfunded post-retirement/severance benefits liability of the school corporation. If such a fund is established it is designated by the State Board of Accounts and the State Department of Local Government Finance as Fund No. 063. Under Indiana law, if this fund is established, the school corporation must fund on an actuarially sound basis the post-retirement or severance benefits created by the collective bargaining agreement or other contract or the increase in the unfunded liability. There is no levy or tax rate permitted for the post-retirement/severance future benefits fund, but this fund must be funded by the school corporation's general fund or rainy day fund. Every expenditure out of the post-retirement/severance future benefits fund must be included within an appropriation approved by the State Department of Local Government Finance.

K. Construction Fund

A school corporation may establish and operate a construction fund whenever funds are received by the school corporation by issuing general obligation bonds or executing a building lease with a building corporation. If such a fund is established it is designated by the State Board of Accounts and the State Department of Local Government Finance as Fund No. 070. The school corporation deposits the money it receives by issuing the general obligation bonds or entering into the lease into the construction fund and uses the money deposited into the construction fund to pay for all or a portion of the projects to be financed by the general obligation bonds or the lease. There is no levy or tax rate permitted for the construction fund. Every expenditure out of the construction fund must be included within an appropriation approved by the State Department of Local Government Finance.

L. School Lunch Fund

A school corporation must establish and operate a school lunch fund, which is designated by the State Board of Accounts and the State Department of Local Government Finance as Fund No. 080, to be used for the deposit of all money received by the school corporation in the sale of school lunches, federal and state reimbursement for lunches and any other money received by the school corporation in connection with the operation of the school corporation's lunch program. Money deposited into this fund may be used to pay for the costs of personal service, supplies, food and equipment for the school corporation's school lunch program. There is no levy or tax rate permitted for the school lunch fund. So long as no property tax collections are deposited into the school lunch fund, every expenditure out of the school lunch fund must be included within an appropriation reported to the State Department of Local Government Finance, but the approval of such appropriation by the State Department of Local Government Finance is not required.

In lieu of using the school lunch fund, a school corporation may use its extra-curricular accounts for the purpose of the school lunch fund. If the extra-curricular account is used the limitations and procedures for the school lunch fund apply to the extra-curricular account.

K. Textbook Rental Fund

A school corporation must establish and operate a textbook rental fund, which is designated by the State Board of Accounts and the State Department of Local Government Finance as Fund No. 090. All money received for the rental of textbooks and workbooks furnished to students must be deposited into the textbook rental fund. Money deposited into the textbook rental fund may be used to pay for the cost of purchasing or renting textbooks and/or workbooks and repairing textbooks. There is no levy or tax rate permitted for the textbook rental fund, and no appropriation is required for the expenditure of money from the textbook rental fund.

GENERAL FUND REFERENDUM PROCESS

I.   GENERAL

Under Indiana law, a school corporation may file a referendum in which the registered voters in the geographical boundaries of the school corporation approve or deny a request of the school corporation for a special increase in the school corporation's general fund levy which is above the normal general fund levy limitation otherwise permitted by Indiana. If the referendum is approved by a majority of the voters who voted on the issue, then the school corporation will be permitted to levy, beginning in the immediately following calendar year, a special general fund levy in addition to the school corporation's normal general fund levy. This special general fund levy will be levied for only the number of years identified in the referendum, but in no event will this special general fund levy be in existence for more than seven years unless a new referendum is held extending this special general fund levy for additional years up to a maximum of an additional seven years. There is not a limitation on the number of times a school corporation may renew this special general fund levy.

II.   THE QUESTION

The question submitted to the voters in the referendum must read as follows:

"For the (insert number) calendar year or years immediately following the holding of the referendum, shall the school corporation impose a property tax rate that does not exceed (insert amount) cents ($0.__) on each one hundred dollars ($100) of assessed valuation and that is in addition to the school corporation's normal tax rate?"

III.   THE PROCESS

A. State Approval

Before the request for the special general fund levy may be considered by the registered voters, the school corporation must submit the request to the Indiana Department of Local Government Finance for its approval of such referendum under Indiana Code 6-1.1-19-4.5(c), as amended. Upon receiving any such request, the Indiana Department of Local Government Finance will forward the matter on to the School Property Tax Control Board for its evaluation and recommendation. In the course of its evaluation, the School Property Tax Control may require the school corporation to appear before the School Property Tax Control Board at one of its monthly hearings to provide information and answer questions prior to the School Property Tax Control Board voting on a recommendation to the Indiana Department of Local Government Finance. If the School Property Tax Control Board recommends that the Indiana Department of Local Government Finance approve the request for the referendum and the Indiana Department of Local Government Finance agrees with that recommendation and approves the request for the referendum, then the School Property

Tax Control Board will certify the special general fund levy question in accordance with Indiana Code 3-10-9-3 to the county election board of each county in which any part of the school corporation is located.

B. County Certification

1. Upon receiving the certified question from the School Property Tax Control Board, the county clerk of each county in which any part of the school corporation is located will call a meeting of the county election board to make arrangements for the referendum. Under Indiana law, the special general fund levy question must be certified no later than noon (1) sixty days prior to a primary election, if the question is being placed on the primary election ballot or (2) of the first day of August, if the question is being placed on the general election ballot. The referendum will be on the ballot at the primary or general election immediately following the certification.

2. However, if the primary or general election immediately following the certification would be more than six months after the referendum is approved by the Indiana Department of Local Government Finance, then the school corporation must hold a special election on the referendum not less than ninety days after the special general fund levy question is certified by the School Property Tax Control Board. If a special election is held, the school corporation will advise the county election board or boards of the date on which it prefers to hold the special election, and, if practicable, the county election board or boards will hold the special election on that date. In addition, the county election board may adopt orders specifying when the registration period for the special election begins and ends. If a special election is held for the referendum, then the costs of the special election must be paid by the school corporation.

C. Public Notice

Not less than ten days before the date scheduled for the referendum, the county election board is required under Indiana law to publish the referendum question in one or two newspapers which are generally circulated or published in the geographical boundaries of the school corporation.

D. Referendum Results

1. At the conclusion of the election, each precinct election board will count the votes in favor and the votes against the referendum and certify those individual totals to the county election board of each county in which the referendum is held. The circuit court clerk of each county will certify the results to the School Property Tax Control Board immediately after the referendum votes have been counted by the election boards. Upon receiving the certification of all of the votes cast in the referendum, the School Property Tax Control Board will promptly certify the results of the referendum to the Indiana Department of Local Government Finance.

GENERAL FUND REFERENDUM PROCESS

2. If a majority of the voters in the referendum voted "yes" on the referendum question, the Indiana Department of Local Government Finance must take prompt and appropriate steps to notify the school corporation that the school corporation is authorized to collect a general fund tax levy in the amount approved by the voters in the referendum in addition to its normal general fund levy for the ensuing calendar year and for the years set forth in the referendum. In the ensuing calendar year, the school corporation will establish a referendum tax levy fund under Indiana 21-2-11.6, as amended, and deposit into the referendum tax levy fund all of the money collected as a result of the special general fund tax levy. A school corporation's referendum tax levy may not be considered in the determination of the school corporation's state tuition support or the determination of the school corporation's maximum normal general fund tax levy.

3. If a majority of the voters in the referendum did not vote "yes" on the referendum question, the Indiana Department of Local Government Finance must take prompt and appropriate steps to notify the school corporation that the school corporation is not authorized to collect a general fund tax levy which is in addition to its normal general fund tax levy, and the school corporation may not hold another special general fund levy referendum for at least one year from the date of the current referendum.

PART IV

BARGAINING

COLLECTIVE BARGAINING IN INDIANA PUBLIC SCHOOLS • UNFAIR PRACTICES

COLLECTIVE BARGAINING IN INDIANA PUBLIC SCHOOLS

I. THE RIGHT TO BARGAIN COLLECTIVELY

Under Indiana law, public employees have no common law or court-created right to engage in collective bargaining. That does not prohibit either (1) school boards from voluntarily engaging in collective bargaining with groups of its employees, or (2) the Indiana General Assembly from passing laws granting bargaining rights to groups of public employees. In Indiana, public employees are prohibited from striking or engaging in any concerted work stoppage.

A. Voluntary collective bargaining

Historically, some school boards across Indiana have chosen to voluntarily recognize and bargain with bargaining agents selected by different groups of employees such as bus drivers, maintenance workers and cafeteria workers. School boards have the right to enter into collective bargaining agreements with those bargaining agents but the law allows school boards to refuse to do so - even if there has been a long history of bargaining contracts with a particular bargaining agent. Thus, while a school board cannot abrogate a collective bargaining agreement during its term, when the agreement expires, the school board can refuse to bargain a new contract.

B. The Collective Bargaining Law

In 1973, with the enactment of Public Law 217 (the "Certified Educational Employee Bargaining Act" or "CEEBA"), the Indiana General Assembly authorized collective bargaining for certified employees of school corporations. (Indiana Code 20-29-1 et seq.) "Certified employees" are defined as people whose contract with a school corporation "requires that he hold a license or permit from the state board of education or commission thereof as provided in Indiana Code 20-28."

C. Charter Schools

Certified employees of a charter school established under Indiana Code 20-24 are expressly authorized to organize and bargain collectively. They enjoy the same rights as certified employees working at public schools under CEEBA. Teachers in a conversion charter school remain part of the unit of the sponsor school and are covered by the collective bargaining agreement in effect at that sponsoring school.

PART IV: BARGAINING

II. ISSUES RELATED TO VOLUNTARY COLLECTIVE BARGAINING

A. Selection of a Bargaining Agent Through Voluntary Recognition

Because there is no established legal mechanism for groups of public employees in a voluntary collective bargaining arrangement to select a bargaining agent, employees typically resort to either "card signing", petitioning the school board or secret ballot election as the means of deciding whether a particular bargaining agent should be selected.

1.   "Card Signing" is simply an authorization card that a majority of the employees in a particular employee group, which is interested in aligning with a union, execute and present to the school administration or school board. The authorization card states that the employee executing it authorizes a particular union to represent him or her in collective bargaining. Sometimes these cards also include a statement that the employee is actually joining the union and will pay dues to it. If less than a majority of the group sign, a school should refuse to recognize the proposed bargaining agent.

2.   A petition is a signup sheet that includes an authorization statement at the beginning of the petition authorizing a union to represent those employees who sign the petition. Sometimes the petition also includes a statement that the employees signing it are also joining the union and will pay dues to it. Again, a majority of the group must indicate their selection of the proposed bargaining agent for the school board to recognize that agent.

3.   A secret ballot election can occur in a variety of ways as permitted by the school corporation. There may be election observers and the election itself may occur after or during working hours in any manner agreed upon by the union and the school board. School boards should refuse to bargain with any proposed bargaining representative that fails to win a majority of the entire group without regard to how many teachers actually vote.

B. Terms of a Collective Bargaining Agreement in a Voluntary Collective Bargaining Arrangement

Once a school board voluntarily recognizes a union, the collective bargaining process begins. During negotiations the union generally will seek to have included in the collective bargaining agreement as many terms and conditions as possible. Typically the agreement will include wages, fringe benefits, layoff and recall procedures, and other terms and conditions of employment.

One of the most sought-after provisions by unions is a grievance process that culminates in binding arbitration. Binding arbitration may be an acceptable method of resolving disputes, but school boards should normally avoid such a provision because it takes the final decision over employment issues away from the school board whose primary mandate is to operate its public schools efficiently. An arbitrator does not sit in the same seat as a school board in this regard.

COLLECTIVE BARGAINING IN INDIANA PULIC SCHOOLS

III. COLLECTIVE BARGAINING FOR CERTIFIED EMPLOYEES UNDER CEEBA

A. The Enforcing Agency

CEEBA contains the requirements imposed on school boards with respect to the collective bargaining process under CEEBA and the means by which CEEBA is enforced. Under CEEBA, the Indiana Education Employment Relations Board ("IEERB") serves as the governing body to implement the law with essentially four primary objectives:

1. Provide a process to determine the appropriate unit and the method that certified employees of school corporations can select (or deselect) an exclusive representative for purposes of engaging in collective bargaining;

2. Provide a method of handling disputes arising from the collective bargaining process;

3. Provide a process for resolving unfair practices allegedly committed by either the school corporation or the exclusive representative; and

4. Account for the activities of the IEERB, school corporations and exclusive representatives. The specific powers provided to the IEERB in order to accomplish these objectives are set forth in Indiana Code 20-7.5-3.

B. The Process For Establishing the Appropriate Unit under CEEBA

There are two methods of establishing the appropriate unit. First, the exclusive representative and the school corporation may agree upon the appropriate unit. If no agreement is reached, then IEERB will determine the appropriate unit after a hearing in which IEERB will consider:

1. The efficient administration of school operations;

2. The existence of a "community of interest" among the school employees;

3. The effects fragmented units would have on the school corporation and school employees; and

4. The recommendations of the parties involved.

The law specifically prohibits non-certificated employees from being part of the appropriate unit comprised of certificated employees. I.C. 20-29-5-1.

PART IV: BARGAINING

C. The Process For Selecting or Deselecting an Exclusive Representative under CEEBA

1. Voluntary Recognition Based on Evidence of Representation

    The school corporation <u>may</u> recognize any exclusive representative who requests to represent a unit of certified employees and presents sufficient evidence to the school corporation of its representative status. Such evidence may be through a showing of interest of signed cards or a petition or other evidence that establishes a majority of the appropriate unit of certified employees want the exclusive representative as their bargaining agent.

    If the school corporation believes the evidence presented to it is sufficient to recognize an exclusive representative, the school corporation must post for thirty days a public notice in each building where the school employees of the appropriate unit principally work stating the school employee organization will be recognized by the school corporation as the exclusive representative of the appropriate unit. However, if the school corporation <u>does not</u> believe the evidence presented to it is sufficient to recognize an exclusive representative, the school corporation must file a petition with the IEERB asserting either (a) one or more school employee organizations have presented to the school corporation a claim for recognition as the exclusive representative of an appropriate unit, or (b) the school corporation has good faith doubt that the school employee organization represents a majority of the employees in the appropriate unit.

    A school corporation <u>cannot</u> recognize a school employee organization as the exclusive representative if, during the thirty day notice period described above, either (a) another organization representing at least twenty percent of the school employees in the unit files a written objection with the IEERB to that recognition request, or (b) any school employee in the unit files a complaint as to the composition of the unit with the school corporation or the IEERB.

2. Other Petitions Which Might Arise during the Representation Process

    In addition to the methods discussed in Section C.1. above, the IEERB election process may be initiated at anytime through an employee petition filed with the IEERB. For such a petition to be sufficient, it must (a) be signed by at least twenty percent of the employees in the appropriate unit and (b) assert either that (i) those employees do not wish to be represented by that organization or (ii) the designated exclusive representative is no longer the representative for a majority of school employees in the appropriate unit.

    Another method to initiate the IEERB election process is through a petition filed by a competing organization with the IEERB asserting (a) that at least twenty percent of the employees in the unit wish to be represented by that organization, or (b) that the designated exclusive representative is no longer the representative for a majority of school employees in the unit.

3.   An Election To Determine Representative Status

Upon receipt of any such petition described in Section C.1. or C.2., above, the IEERB will investigate the petition to determine if it has reasonable cause to believe a question exists whether the existing designated exclusive representative or any school employee organization represents a majority of the school employees in the appropriate unit. If so, a hearing will be held within thirty days. Based on the record presented at that hearing, the IEERB will determine whether a secret ballot election for the selection of an exclusive representative within the appropriate unit will proceed.

Critically, to win, a school employee organization must win a majority vote of all employees in the unit rather than a majority of those voting. For example, if the appropriate unit is comprised of one hundred teachers only seventy of whom actually vote, fifty-one must vote in favor of a particular school employee organization for it to be designated as the exclusive representative of the appropriate unit. No vote is permitted within twenty-four months after a valid election occurs.

The details of the election including such things as time, place and manner of voting, permitted campaign activities, and what is in the ballot are all issues resolved by the IEERB.

D. Issues Arising in the Collective Bargaining Process under CEEBA

1.   Negotiations

In negotiating a collective bargaining agreement, CEEBA identifies that the school corporation has express authority and responsibility to (a) direct the work of its employees; (b) establish policies consistent with the school corporation's bargaining and discussion obligations; (c) hire, promote, demote, transfer, assign, retain, layoff, discipline, suspend and discharge employees consistent with the school corporation's bargaining and discussion obligations; (d) maintain the efficiency of school corporation's operations; and (e) take actions necessary to carry out the mission of the public schools.

Thus, while the negotiation process may result in some limitations on the school corporation in its ability to act, the law specifically permits the school corporation to retain broad authority to run the school system. However, it is unlawful for the parties to reach an agreement that causes the school corporation to engage in deficit financing (which means expending more money than is available to the school corporation in any budget year.)

2.   Bargaining Collectively vs. Discussion under CEEBA

Quite different from private sector law governing negotiations of unions with private sector employers under the National Labor Relations Act, Indiana school corporations are not required to bargain to impasse the wide range of issues that typically comprise the "terms and conditions" of employment. The obligation of school corporations to bargain collectively is significantly different from the obligation of discussion under Indiana law.

"Bargaining collectively" requires the school corporation and the exclusive representative to meet at reasonable times to negotiate in good faith with respect to subjects of bargaining and to execute a written contract incorporating those matters upon which agreement has been reached. The school corporation is not required to either agree to a specific proposal or make a concession of any kind. Bargainable issues <u>are</u> subject to the impasse procedures described below.

"Discussion" requires the school corporation and the exclusive representative to meet at reasonable times (a) to discuss; (b) to provide meaningful input; and (c) to exchange point of view on the subjects of discussion. Discussion issues <u>are not</u> subject to impasse procedures.

3.   Subjects of Bargaining under CEEBA

Bargainable issues (commonly referred to as "Section 4 issues") are defined under Indiana Code 20-29-6-4 to include: salary, wages, hours, and salary and wage related fringe benefits. In addition, items included in the 1972-1973 bargaining agreements (even though not falling within the defined economic issues above) are also treated as bargainable issues under Indiana Code 20-29-6-7(c).

4.   Subjects of Discussion under CEEBA.

Issues that must be discussed by school corporations with the exclusive representative (commonly referred to as "Section 5 issues") include (a) working conditions that are not subject to bargaining; (b) curriculum development and revision; (c) textbook selection; (d) teaching methods; (e) hiring, promotion, demotion, transfer, assignment and retention of certificated employees as well as any change to the statutory rights of certified employees under the "Teacher Tenure Law" (Indiana Code 20-28-6); (f) student discipline, including expulsion or supervision of students; (g) pupil-teacher ratio; and (h) class size or budget appropriations.

COLLECTIVE BARGAINING IN INDIANA PULIC SCHOOLS

5.   The Process of Bargaining under CEEBA

Bargaining itself has been described by some as more an art than a science. Meeting with the exclusive representative in good faith to reach a mutual understanding over the terms of a new contract can be as simple as exchanging ideas and then agreeing to terms in one or two meetings or as difficult as the parties wish to make it by disagreeing over even the most mundane issues such as where and when the negotiation meetings are to occur. Personalities sometime enter into the equation. The following is a short list of helpful hints on successful bargaining.

(1)   Have the right bargaining team. Credibility and professionalism mean everything. If the union negotiators distrust or resent members of the school corporation's team, it is much more difficult to reach agreement than if a level of trust exists.

(2)   Be prepared - good things happen when preparation meets opportunity. School corporation representatives should have a thorough working knowledge of all aspects of the school corporation's proposal and the anticipated union's proposal.

(3)   Be aware of outside influences and be ready to respond to them. School board members should have confidence in the school corporation's representatives and be willing to defer all questions about negotiations to them, notwithstanding any relationship board member(s) may have with any teachers. Moreover it is generally best that the school board not fight a war in the press and negotiate the contract in public.

(4)   Be smart on language issues. Use understandable terms to describe what is agreeable to both sides. Poor grammar, confusing or complicated language, or simply not saying what you mean, can only lead to misunderstandings.

(5)   End negotiations on a high note. Position the school corporation so it can give the last thing the union negotiators want. Walking away from the table with a handshake and a desire to work together will hopefully result in a positive working relationship for the rest of the school year(s).

If negotiations do not result in the parties reaching a collective bargaining agreement, the law requires the parties to maintain the "status quo" and tentative contracts can be issued by the school corporation to certificated employees. This means that the same terms and conditions remain in effect unless both parties agree otherwise. This can have a dramatic effect on the school corporation and the employees alike. For example, the economic impact of maintaining the "status quo" in school corporations that have salary schedules based on years of teaching credit is that teachers who are not at the top of the salary scale receive an "increment" raise at the beginning of each school year. If health care and/or health insurance contributions by the school district are fixed in amount, the burden of increased premiums would fall on the covered employee. If a percentage contribution is applied under the previous contract, the same percentage is used for any change in premiums.

6. Timetable for Bargaining under CEEBA

Statutorily, bargaining should begin one hundred eighty days before the school corporation publishes the school corporation's budget as required in Indiana Code 6-11-17-3 (the "submission date"). The law also states that a party may declare an impasse and utilize the impasse procedures at any time after the 180-day period has commenced. If an agreement on the bargainable issues is not reached within seventy-five days before the submission date, the IEERB is required to initiate mediation with a mediator selected by the IEERB. If an agreement over bargainable issues is not reached within forty-five days before the submission date, the IEERB is to initiate fact-finding.

7. Impasse procedures under CEEBA

(1) Mediation. The IEERB has the authority to appoint a mediator to resolve open issues in the negotiations. A mediator does not have the ability to require either party to settle on any specific term. Rather, a mediator is used to find solutions and to provide opportunities for the parties to reach common ground on as many issues as possible. Mediation is a confidential process, and a mediator cannot be subpoenaed by any court or administrative agency with respect to any matter that was discussed as part of the mediation process.

(2) Fact-Finding. Fact-finding is a process utilized to provide a neutral advisory opinion on bargainable issues left unresolved in the negotiation process. The IEERB selects the fact-finder who may hold such hearings as the fact-finder deems appropriate to understand and then provide recommendations as to the outstanding issues. Because matters of discussion are not subject to impasse procedures, either party may refuse to submit discussion issues to the fact-finder.

In making his or her recommendations, the fact-finder takes into consideration (i) past agreements of the parties; (ii) comparisons of wages and hours of the employees involved with those of other employees at other public agencies and private organizations doing comparable work; (iii) the public interest; and (iv) the financial impact on the school corporation - particularly if any settlement would result in deficit financing.

The fact-finder issues his written recommendations to the parties and the IEERB. The IEERB may make those recommendations available to the public within five (5) days after issuance but must make them available to the public through the news media and other sources not later than ten (10) days after issuance.

(3)   Arbitration. The parties may agree to binding arbitration as to any or all of the issues left unresolved in the bargaining process but are not required to do so.

UNFAIR PRACTICES

HANDLING AND RESOLVING UNFAIR PRACTICES RELATED TO BARGAINING

A. The Ongoing Obligation to Bargain or Discuss

Under Indiana law, there is a continuing obligation on the part of a school corporation to bargain or discuss issues that arise during the term of a labor agreement. This obligation arises when changes in the working conditions occur and specific language in the labor agreement does not address those changes. Whether an issue is the subject of a bargaining obligation or a discussion obligation determines how a school corporation has to deal with the matter. When a school corporation fails to timely address a change with the exclusive representative or fails to meet its bargaining obligation with respect to an issue, such failure may give rise to an unfair practice filing by the exclusive representative.

B. Unfair Practices

1. Under Indiana Code 20-29-7, it is an unfair practice for a school corporation to interfere with, restrain or coerce school corporation employees in the exercise of their rights under CEEBA. Unfair practices may include actions on the part of the school corporation that do not relate to collective bargaining issues. However, it is expressly an unfair practice to refuse to bargain collectively or discuss with an exclusive representative as required by law.

2. Issues that must be bargained include salary, wages, hours, and salary and wage related fringe benefits. Health insurance benefits must be bargained. In addition, items such as a "wellness program", maternity leave and sick leave are also subject to bargaining.

3. The first issue to address in the school corporation's duty to discuss obligation is, "Who is responsible to initiate discussion?" The answer is that it depends. Generally speaking, if the exclusive representative is aware of an issue, it is incumbent upon the exclusive representative to initiate discussion. If, on the other hand, the school corporation is going to change a past practice e.g. a course of conduct over a period of time, it is up to the school corporation to initiate discussion on the change. For example, where a school corporation has paid make-up days by issuing supplemental contracts at the end of a school year, the school corporation is required to initiate discussion before deciding not to pay for make-up days in following years. Items that must be discussed by a school corporation are listed in Indiana Code 20-29-6-7.

C. Past Practice

Past practice can be a double edge sword. On the one hand, the exclusive representative can rely on past practice to contest changes by the school corporation where no discussion has occurred. On the other hand, the school corporation may be able to rely on past practice such as utilizing the decision of a joint health insurance committee comprised of some teacher representatives to avoid an otherwise required bargaining obligation. Due to the unique factual settings of failure to discuss/failure to bargain claims, school corporations need to evaluate the merits of each situation independently.

D. Discriminatory Actions

1. The types of conduct that can get a school employer in trouble include refusing to bargain about Section 4 issues or refusing or failing to discuss Section 5 issues. Differentiating which issues are subject to the obligation to bargain as opposed to obligation to discuss can be difficult. In addition to wages, hours and economic fringe benefits expressly described in Indiana Code 20-29-6-4, bargainable issues of school corporations which had a comprehensive labor contract in the 1972-1973 school year include language issues addressed in that labor contract. Care must be taken to determine ahead of time whether a matter is subject to negotiation or subject to discussion.

2. IEERB cases

    Because the facts and circumstances in each case are determinative as to whether a school corporation violated its bargaining or discussion obligation under CEEBA, it is not practical to list the resolution of each case in these materials. Cases addressed by the IEERB can be found online at <u>www.in.gov/ieerb/cases.</u> Nevertheless, an example of how the IEERB has previously addressed just one issue (group health insurance) can be instructive as to the complications that school corporations face in meeting their obligation to bargain or discuss issues with the exclusive representative for the teachers.

    In <u>Goshen Education Assn et al and Board of Trustees of Goshen Community Schools</u>, Case No. U-00-03-2315, the school corporation was found to have violated CEEBA by unilaterally changing a past practice when it used reinsurance reimbursements to make three monthly premium payments instead of making such premium payments from the school corporation's general fund as it had a practice of doing. On the other hand, in <u>Goodwin and Board of Trustees of Mount Pleasant Township Community School Corp.</u>, Case no. U-98-02-1910, where a joint insurance committee comprised of teacher representatives and school representatives resolved changes in the health care plan, the teacher association was found to have waived its right to bargain over such changes because it acquiesed in the parties past practice of dealing with health plan issues through the insurance committee.

UNFAIR PRACTICES

E. Process for Resolving Unfair Practices

1.   A school corporation or any school employee aggrieved by an alleged unfair practice may file an unfair practice complaint with the IEERB to seek redress. The complaint must (a) be under oath, (b) set out a summary of facts involved, and (c) include the specific section or sections of CEEBA allegedly violated.

2.   Upon receipt of the unfair practice complaint, the IEERB gives notice to the opposing party of the complaint and a hearing is scheduled before a hearing examiner assigned by the IEERB. Individuals may be subpoenaed to attend the hearing at which testimony is taken. The IEERB may also issue subpoenas for documents and other things. Failure to comply with subpoenas may result in the IEERB seeking enforcement in state court. Parties may be represented by counsel at the unfair practice hearing, a transcript is made of the hearing and parties are entitled to cross examine witnesses. It is typical for the parties to submit post hearing briefs in support of their positions. The hearing examiner makes findings of fact and conclusions of law that are submitted to the IEERB for review and adoption.

3.   The IEERB has the power to revise the hearing examiner's findings and to issue such interlocutory orders as it deems necessary to carry out the intent of CEEBA. The IEERB's determination is final and may be appealed to the Indiana Court of Appeals which will review the IEERB's decision to determine whether it is supported in the law.

F. Helpful References

Set forth below are a list of websites which you may wish to access for further information on school employment related issues:

1.   www.in.gov/laws for Indiana statutes;

2.   www.in.gov/ieerb/cases for the Indiana Education Employment Relations Board;

3.   www.isba.org for the Indiana School Boards Association; and

4.   www.ista.org for the Indiana State Teachers Association.

ARTICLE II

ABC's OF SCHOOL LAW

ALPHABETICAL QUICK REFERENCE
FOR
SCHOOL ADMINISTRATORS

CONTENTS AT A GLANCE

A

ADMINISTRATION

ATTENDANCE

B

BOARDS OF EDUCATION

BUILDING PROJECTS, BOR-
    ROWING, BUDGETS &
    BARGAINING

C

CENSORSHIP

CHILD ABUSE REPORTING

COLLECTIVE BARGAINING

COMPULSORY ATTENDANCE

CONTRACTS

CORPORAL PUNISHMENT

D

DISCIPLINE

DRUGS & DRUG TESTING

E

EMPLOYEE EVALUATION

EQUAL EDUCATIONAL
    OPPORTUNITIES ACT

EXPULSIONS & EXCLUSIONS

F

FAMILY RIGHTS & PRIVACY
    ACT

FIELD TRIPS

FINANCE

FREEDOM OF EXPRESSION

FREEDOM OF RELIGION

G

GANGS & GANG ACTIVITY

H

HOME RULE

HOME SCHOOLING

I–K

IMMUNITY

IMMUNIZATIONS

INTERNET USAGE

L

LEGAL SETTLEMENT

LICENSURE

M–N

MEDICAL & MEDICINES

NEGLIGENCE

O–P

PRAYER

PROCEDURAL DUE PROCESS

Q–S

SEARCH & SEIZURE

T

TEACHER DISMISSAL

TEACHER RECORDS

TENURE

TITLE IX

TORT LIABILITY

TRANSPORTATION

U–V

VACCINATIONS

VOLUNTEERS

W–Z

WAIVERS

WITHDRAWAL

ABC's OF SCHOOL LAW

<u>ADMINISTRATION:</u> IC 20-28; See Chapter Four in the main text

POINTS OF EMPHASIS:

I. PRINCIPAL, ASSISTANT PRINCIPAL AND ASSISTANT SUPERINTENDENT CONTRACTS

A. Principal, assistant principal or assistant superintendent contracts are to be on the regular teacher's contract prescribed by the state superintendent of public instruction.

B. The contract shall be the equivalent of two (2) school years, but can be more than two years if acceptable to the principal and the school board.

C. The contract can be modified at any time during the term if agreed to by both parties.

D. Assistant superintendents, principals and assistant principals must be notified by February of the year during which the contract is to expire. If no notification is made the contract shall be in force for the ensuing school year.

E. The school board or its designee must notify the principal, assistant principal or assistant superintendent thirty (30) days before giving written notice of refusal to renew a contract.

F. If the principal, assistant principal or assistant superintendent is properly notified of non renewal intentions, he/she has the right to ask for a private conference with the superintendent within five (5) days after receiving notification.

G. The principal, assistant principal or assistant superintendent then has a right to request and receive a private meeting with the school board within five (5) days after the initial private conversation with the superintendent.

H. The rights of a principal, assistant principal, or assistant superintendent as a teacher under any other laws are not affected.

II. SUPERINTENDENT CONTRACTS

A. The basic contract is in the form of the regular teacher's contract.

B. The contract is for a term of at least thirty-six (36) months.

C. The contract can be modified at any time by mutual consent.

D. The rights of a superintendent as a teacher under any other laws are not affected.

E. If contract is to be terminated the school board must give proper notice and the superintendent can request a hearing ten (10) days before the termination. The hearing must be granted in an official meeting if requested.

ALPHABETICAL QUICK REFERENCE FOR SCHOOL ADMINISTRATORS   115

F. The superintendent must be notified on or before January 1 of the year the contract expires or will not be renewed.

G. If proper notification is not made, the contract is extended for twelve (12) months.

III.   ANTI-DISCRIMINATION; RESIDENCE REQUIREMENTS

A. A school board may not adopt residence requirements for teachers or other school employees. Each school corporation that fails to observe this restriction is ineligible for state funds.

ATTENDANCE: IC 20-33-2; See Chapter Eleven in the main text

POINTS OF EMPHASIS:

A. The school board must adopt a procedure affording a parent of an individual who does not meet the minimum age requirement the right to appeal to the superintendent of the school corporation for enrollment of the individual in kindergarten at an age earlier than the age.

B. A student who is at least 16 years old but less than 18 is bound by the requirements of compulsory school attendance and may not withdraw from school before graduation unless:

1.   the student, the student's parent or guardian, and the principal agree to the withdrawal; and

2.   at the exit interview, the student provides written acknowledgement of the withdrawal and the student's parent or guardian and the principal each provide written consent for the student to withdraw from school.

C. The school board must designate the appropriate employees of the school corporation to conduct the exit interviews for students. Each exit interview must be personally attended by:

1.   the student's parent or guardian;

2.   the student;

3.   each designated appropriate school employee; and

4.   the student's principal.

D. Each public school and each private school may require a student who initially enrolls in the school to provide:

1.   the name and address of the school the student last attended; and

2.   a certified copy of the student's birth certificate or other reliable proof of the student's date of birth.

If the documentation is not provided within thirty (30) days or appears to be fraudulent, the school must notify the Indiana clearinghouse for information on missing children.

E. Each school board must establish and include as a part of the written copy of its discipline rules a definition of a student who is habitually truant. Under this definition the student may not be issued an operator's license or a learner's permit to drive a motor vehicle or motorcycle until the person is at least 18 years of age.

F. Upon review, the school board may determine that the person's attendance record has improved to the degree that the person may become eligible to be issued an operator's license or a learner's permit.

G. Before February 1 and before October 1 each year, the school board must submit to the bureau of motor vehicles the pertinent information concerning a person's eligibility to be issued the license or permit.

H. A student is excused from attending school for any of the following reasons:

1. service as a page or as an honoree of the Indiana general assembly; this applies to ALL pupils, whether they attend public, private or parochial schools;

2. service on precinct election board;

3. issued a subpoena to appear in court;

4. ordered to active duty in the Indiana National Guard (for not more than ten (10) days in a school year);

5. is appointed to state standards task force; or

6. religious instruction not to exceed one hundred twenty (120) aggregate minutes in any week.

I. An accurate daily record of the attendance of each child who is subject to compulsory school attendance must be kept by every public and private school.

J. Within fifteen (15) school days after the beginning of each semester, the principal of every public high school must send to the superintendent a list of names and last known addresses of all students who did not graduate during the prior semester and not enrolled in the then current semester.

ALPHABETICAL QUICK REFERENCE FOR SCHOOL ADMINISTRATORS   117

K. When a truant child is delivered to a principal during a school day the child will NOT be kept at school beyond the regular hour of dismissal on that day and as promptly as possible the parents must be notified by phone or by mail the same day the principal receives the child.

L. Students cannot be denied enrollment because of no specific documentation on residence.

BOARD OF EDUCATION: IC 20-26; See Chapter One in the main text

POINTS OF EMPHASIS:

A. The school corporation has all powers granted it by statute or through rules adopted by state board of education and all other powers necessary or desirable in the conduct of its affairs, even though not granted by statute or rule (Home Rule).

B. If there is no constitutional or statutory provision requiring a specific manner for exercising a power, a school corporation wanting to exercise the power must adopt a written policy for exercising the power.

C. The state and other agencies may review or regulate the exercise of powers by a school corporation only to the extent prescribed by statute.

D. The school corporation must provide a latch key program either in the school or contract with a not-for-profit organization.

E. The school corporation may adopt a policy to provide athletic tickets at reduced or no charge to groups or individuals designated by the school board.

F. The school corporation may appropriate necessary funds to provide memberships to state and national associations and may also appropriate necessary funds to defray expenses of attending meetings for these organizations.

G. The school corporation must adopt a policy on criminal records checks, administer them uniformly and the individual is responsible for all costs in obtaining these checks.

H. School board members can be paid up to $2000 per year plus a per diem not to exceed the rate approved for members of the board of school commissioners.

I. School board members cannot be disqualified on the basis of age if at least 21 years of age.

J. School board members do not have to own land, but must reside in the school corporation.

K. School board members cannot be an individual who is employed by the school corporation.

ALPHABETICAL QUICK REFERENCE FOR SCHOOL ADMINISTRATORS   119

BUILDING PROJECTS, BORROWING, BUDGETS AND BARGAINING: See Article I in the supplement

B

120   ABC's OF SCHOOL LAW

CENSORSHIP: See Chapter Eight in the main text

POINTS OF EMPHASIS:

A. A school corporation may use any excerpt of the 15 American history or heritage documents defined by Indiana Code.

B. A school corporation may not permit the content-based censorship of American history or heritage based on religious references in the 15 American history or heritage documents in accordance with Indiana Code.

C. If a student uses excerpts from any of the 15 American history or heritage documents defined by Indiana Code the student may not be punished in any way, including a reduction in grade.

D. A library, media center or an equivalent facility that a school corporation maintains for student use must contain in the facility's permanent collection at least one (1) copy of each of the 15 American history or heritage documents defined by Indiana Code.

E. A forum analysis should be performed by the building administrator before using censorship.

F. Local decisions about curriculum, books and materials may be made on the basis of school board decisions.

G. Censorship should relate to legitimate pedagogical concerns.

H. Broad latitude exists to protect school children from harmful influences, especially as it relates to obscenity and sex.

I. Instructional programming policies should exist for the selection of curricula, books and materials.

CHILD ABUSE REPORTING: IC 31-32-11-1, IC 31-33-1-1 et seq. and IC 31-34-1-1 et seq.

POINTS OF EMPHASIS:

A. In service all staff yearly concerning child abuse and neglect reporting requirements also include training to recognize the signs of child abuse and neglect.

B. School corporations are required to cooperate with the local child protection service.

C. All school corporation personnel who have ***reason to believe*** that a child is a victim of child abuse or neglect **must** immediately notify the building principal.

ALPHABETICAL QUICK REFERENCE FOR SCHOOL ADMINISTRATORS 121

D. The building principal **must** immediately make an oral report to the local child protection service or the local law enforcement agency.

E. People required to report are immune from civil or criminal liability.

F. A person who is required to make a report and fails to do so is guilty of a Class B misdemeanor.

G Child abuse and/or neglect includes:

1.   Inflicting, or allowing to be inflicted, upon a child physical or emotional injury to the extent that a child needs care, treatment, or rehabilitation;

2.   Not supplying a child with necessary food, clothing, shelter, medical care, education, or supervision to the extent the child's physical or mental condition is seriously impaired or seriously endangered;

3.   Committing or allowing someone to commit a sex offense against a child; or

4.   Negligent treatment or maltreatment under circumstances which indicate that a child's welfare or safety is harmed.

COLLECTIVE BARGAINING (PL 217): IC 20-29; See Chapter Thirteen in the main text

POINTS OF EMPHASIS:

A.   The rights of employees:

1.   To form, join, or assist employee organizations;

2.   To participate in collective bargaining with school employers through representatives of their own choosing; and

3.   To engage in other activities, individually or in concert, for the purpose of establishing, maintaining, or improving salaries, wages, hours, salary and wage related fringe benefits and other defined matters.

B.   The rights of employers:

1.   Direct the work of employees;

2.   Establish policy;

3.   Hire promote, demote, transfer, assign, and retain employees;

4.   Suspend or discharge its employees in accordance with applicable law;

ABC's OF SCHOOL LAW

5. Maintain the efficiency of school operations;

6. Relieve its employees from duties because of lack of work or other legitimate reasons; and

7. Take actions necessary to carry out the mission of the public schools as provided by law.

C. Collective bargaining means negotiations in good faith, and execution of a written contract.

D. Subjects which an employer is required to bargain (known as Section 4 items):

1. salary;

2. wages;

3. hours; and

4. salary and wage-related fringe benefits.

E. Subjects which an employer is required to discuss (known as Section 5 items):

1. all working conditions;

2. curriculum development and revision;

3. textbook selection;

4. teaching methods;

5. hiring, promotion, demotion, transfer, assignment, and retention of teachers;

6. student discipline;

7. expulsion or supervision of students;

8. pupil-teacher ratio; and

9. class size or budget appropriations.

F. The administrative staff must be familiar with the master contract for terms and conditions.

COMPULSORY ATTENDANCE: See Attendance

ALPHABETICAL QUICK REFERENCE FOR SCHOOL ADMINISTRATORS 123

CONTRACTS: IC 20-26-4-8, IC 20-27-5-2 et seq., IC 20-28-6-1 et seq. and IC 20-30-15-6 et seq.; See Chapter Three, Chapter Four and Chapter Five in the main text

POINTS OF EMPHASIS:

A. Check to make sure certificated staff have valid license before contract is signed.

B. Use the contracts prescribed by State Superintendent of Public Instruction for certificated employees.

C. Use forms prescribed by school board policy for non-certificated employees.

D. Non-certificated employees are generally considered at-will and may be terminated for cause at any time.

E. All certificated administrators are covered under tenure laws and employment counts toward teacher tenure.

CORPORAL PUNISHMENT: See Chapter Six in the main text and Discipline in this Article II of the supplement.

POINTS OF EMPHASIS:

A. In Indiana corporal punishment is allowed by law, but each school corporation has the duty and right to adopt policy and/or administrative guidelines to limit or prohibit the use of corporal punishment.

ABC's OF SCHOOL LAW

<u>DISCIPLINE:</u> IC 20-33-8-1 et seq., IC 31-34-1-7, IC 33-9-5, IC 33-9-6, IC 34-13-3-3 & 19, IC 35-47-1-5 and I.C. 35-41-1-8; See Chapter Three and Chapter Six in the main text

POINTS OF EMPHASIS:

A. The school board must establish written discipline rules, which may include dress codes, that govern the conduct of the students, and the school board must give general publicity to the written discipline rules by either making them available or delivering a written copy of the rules to the students and parents.

B. When drafting or reviewing student discipline rules, administrators and board members should be aware of U.S. constitutional concepts that are applicable to student discipline rules.

    1.   Procedural due process.

    2.   Free speech.

    3.   Vagueness and overbreadth.

C. Items that are required to be included in the student handbook are:

    1.   Medication for chronic illness;

    2.   Habitual truancy; and

    3.   Revocation of driver's license or learner's permit.

D. Statutory grounds for suspension and expulsion include:

    1.   Possession of a firearm, a destructive device, or a deadly weapon on school grounds or at school sponsored activities;

    2.   Unlawful activity on or off school grounds, committed during weekends, holidays, school breaks, and summer when a student may not be attending school functions, if the unlawful activity may reasonably be considered to be an interference with school purposes or an education function or the student's removal is necessary to restore order or protect persons on school property;

    3.   Legal settlement; and

    4.   Engaging in misconduct and/or substantial disobedience, as defined by a school or school corporation's written student discipline rules, that occurs:

        (a)   on school property immediately before, during, or immediately after school hours or at any other time when school is being used by a school group;

ALPHABETICAL QUICK REFERENCE FOR SCHOOL ADMINISTRATORS 125

    (b) off school grounds at a school activity, function, or event; or

    (c) traveling to or from school or a school activity, function, or event.

E. Administrators and teachers have other disciplinary powers in addition to suspension, expulsion, and exclusion including:

    1. Reassigning the student to an alternative education setting;

    2. Corporal punishment;

    3. Restriction of extracurricular activities; and

    4. Any additional provision unique to the local situation.

F. School officials have the power to mandate parent participation in any action the school corporation takes to correct a student's behavior.

G. Students cannot be disciplined and/or records refused to be presented because of lack of payment of fees and/or fines.

DRUGS AND DRUG TESTING: IC 7.1-5-7, IC 20-30-5-11, IC 20-33-9-1 et seq., IC 20-34-2-2 et seq., IC 20-34-3-18 and IC 35-48-4; See Chapter Three, Chapter Six and Chapter Seven in the main text

POINTS OF EMPHASIS:

A. Each school corporation is required for each grade from kindergarten through grade 12 to provide instruction concerning the effects alcohol beverages, tobacco, prescription drugs, and controlled substances have on the human body and society at large.

B. The school board is required to establish a drug-free school committee for each school in the school corporation.

C. Each committee must develop a drug-free school plan that includes collecting and reporting drug related activities in the school and addresses ways to eliminate illegal drugs and drug related behavior in schools.

D. School personnel are to report in writing to a member of the administrative staff if they personally observe the use of alcohol or a controlled substance in, on, or within 1,000 feet of school property.

E. The administrative staff is to report the observed violation in writing to a law enforcement officer.

F. The person making the written report is not liable for civil damages or penalties and is presumed to have acted in good faith.

G. The school may not send home medications with a student in grades K-8.

H. The school may send home medication with a student in grades 9-12 if the student's parent provides written permission for the student to receive the medication.

I. Currently, case law has established precedent that drug testing is allowed under certain circumstances.

J. Each school corporation must establish the need and/or desire to establish a random drug testing policy and procedure for the school corporation.

ALPHABETICAL QUICK REFERENCE FOR SCHOOL ADMINISTRATORS 127

EMPLOYEE EVALUATION: IC 20-28-11-1 et seq.; See Chapter Four and Chapter Thirteen in the main text

POINTS OF EMPHASIS:

A. Each school corporation must develop and implement a staff performance evaluation plan to evaluate the performance of each certificated employee.

B. The contents of each plan:

 1. must provide for the improvement of the performance of the individuals evaluated;

 2. must provide for the growth and development of the individuals evaluated;

 3. must provide periodic assessment of the effectiveness of the plan;

 4. must provide that nonpermanent and semi-permanent teachers receive an evaluation on or before December 31 each year, and if requested by the teacher, an additional evaluation on or before March 1 of the following year; and

 5. may provide a basis for making employment decisions.

C. The plan may not provide for an evaluation that is based in whole or in part on the ISTEP test scores of the students in the school corporation.

EQUAL EDUCATIONAL OPPORTUNITIES ACT: IC 30-9-1 et seq.; IC 33-1-1 et seq. and See Chapter Nine in the main text

POINTS OF EMPHASIS:

A. It is the public policy of the state of Indiana to provide, furnish, and make available equal, non-segregated, non-discriminatory educational opportunities and facilities in public schools for all regardless of race, creed, national origin, color, or sex.

B. It is the policy of the state of Indiana to provide bilingual-bicultural programs for all students to:

 1. aid students to reach an acceptable academic level of achievement, and

 2. preserve an awareness of cultural and linguistic heritage.

EXPULSIONS AND EXCLUSIONS: See Chapter Three and Chapter Six in the main text, Discpline in this Article II of the supplement and Procedural Due Process in this Article II of the supplement

ALPHABETICAL QUICK REFERENCE FOR SCHOOL ADMINISTRATORS 129

FAMILY RIGHTS AND PRIVACY ACT: 20 U.S.C. 1232 (Family Rights and Privacy Act of 1974) and IC 20-32-7-6

POINTS OF EMPHASIS:

A. School boards must enact policies to establish a process for the handling of student records.

B. A non-custodial stepparent has no right to access student records. However, a non-custodial parent has the right to access student records.

C. A parent consent is required to disclose the content of a student's portfolio to a perspective employer.

D. School boards must adopt a policy and distribute it to parents on what constitutes directory information in their school corporation and give parents a chance to not allow this directory information to be disseminated.

FIELD TRIPS: See Chapter Two in the main text and Negligence in this Article II of the supplement

FINANCE: See Article I of the supplement

FREEDOM OF EXPRESSION: See Chapter Eight in the main text

POINTS OF EMPHASIS:

A. First Amendment guarantees freedom of speech, press, assembly and religion (establishment clause) and is also included in Indiana Constitution Article 1, Section 3.

B. Students cannot assert a freedom of expression right under the First Amendment of the U.S. Constitution to engage in defamatory, obscene, lewd, or inflammatory expression in public schools. Tinker v. Des Moines Independent School District, 393 U.S. 503 (1969)-Foundation ruling for freedom of expression.

C. Some landmark cases in United States Supreme Court for employers:

1. Pickering v. Board of Education, teachers first amendment rights in matters of public concern;

2. Mt. Healthy City School District v. Doyle, school officials are not prevented from discharging the employee if sufficient cause exists independent of the protected speech;

3. Givhan v. Western Line Consolidated School District, the forum where the expression occurs does not determine whether it is of public or personal interest;

4. Connick v. Meyers, the form and context as well as the content of the expression should be considered in assessing whether it relates to public matters;

5. Bethel School District No. 403 v. Fraser, 106 S. Ct. 3159 (1986);

6. Dodd v. Rambis, 535 F. Supp 23. (1981);

7. Hazelwood School district v. Kuhlmeier, 108 S. Ct. 562 (1988);

8. Melton v. Young, 465 F2d 1332 (6th Cir. 1972) cert. denied, 411 U.S. 951 (1973); and

9. Muller v. Jefferson Lighthouse School, 98 F. 3d 1530 (7th Cir. 1996).

FREEDOM OF RELIGION: IC 20-30-6-12 and IC 20-33-2-19; See Chapter Eight in the main text

POINTS OF EMPHASIS:

A. Establishment Clause in the First Amendment of the U.S. Constitution: "Congress shall make no law respecting an establishment of religion, or prohibiting the free exercise thereof." This is also included in the Indiana Constitution Article 1, Section 3.

B. A parent has a right to be notified of a voluntary religious observance in school and to have his/her child provided an alternative location for study or recreation.

C. A parent may permit his/her child to attend religious instruction up to 120 aggregate minutes per week. This may include religion; however, the request does not ensure approval.

D. A parent may request in writing an exemption from health and hygiene, or sanitary science instruction without penalty for grades and graduation.

E. Landmark Cases in United States Supreme Court:

1. Santa Fe Indep. Sch Dist. V. Doe;

2. Lamb's Chapel v. Center Moriches Unified Sch. Dist., 508 U.S. 384 (1993);

3. Tinker v. Des Moines Independent School District, 393 U.S. 503 (1969);

4. Bd. Of Educ. Of the Westside Community Sch. V. Mergens, 496 U.S. 226 (1990);

ALPHABETICAL QUICK REFERENCE FOR SCHOOL ADMINISTRATORS   131

5.   Engle v. Vitale, 370 U.S. 421 (1962); and

6.   School Dist. Of Abington Twp. v. Schempp, 374 U.S. 203 (1963).

F.   Additional Court decisions:

1.   Engle v. Vitale, 370 U.S. 421 (1962);

2.   McCollum v. Board of Education, 333 U.S. 203 (1948);

3.   Epperson v. Arkansas, 393 U.S. 97, 106 (1968);

4.   Stone v. Graham, 449 U.S. 39 (1980);

5.   Wallace v. Jeffree, 472 U.S. 38 (1985);

6.   Edwards v. Aquillard, 482 U.S. 578 (1987);

7.   Doe v. Shenandoah Cty. Sch. Bd., 737 F. Supp. 913, 918 (W.D. Va. 1990); and

8.   The Good News Club v. Milford Ctr. Sch., 121 S. Ct. 2093 (2001).

Be aware that Amish parents may exempt their child from compulsory attendance laws by withdrawing their child from formal education after eighth grade. U.S. Constitution, First Amendment, Yoder v. Wisconsin, 92 S.Ct. 1526 (1972); Indiana Constitution Article 1, Section 3.

GANGS AND GANG ACTIVITY: IC 34-31-4-2, IC 20-33-8-12, IC 35-45-9-1-2-3-4 and IC 35-43-2-2; See Chapter Six in the main text

POINTS OF EMPHASIS:

A. A school corporation must realize "gangs and gang members" can be misidentified and thus their Constitutional and Civil Rights can be violated. A gang is at least 5 members, which engages in criminal acts that are Class C or D Felonies.

B. Schools may engage in professional development, safety programs and personnel, and drug testing to make schools safer. Olesen v. Bd. Of Education School District 228, 676 F. Supp. 820 (N.D. lll.1987).

C. Schools and school corporations should conduct training/educational sessions on gangs and gang activity in their area.

ALPHABETICAL QUICK REFERENCE FOR SCHOOL ADMINISTRATORS 133

HOME RULE/BOARD OF SCHOOL TRUSTEES: IC 20-26-3, IC 20-26-5-1 and IC 20-26-5-4; See Chapter One in the main text and Board of Education in this Article II of the supplement

POINT OF EMPHASIS:

A. Home Rule means that the school corporation has all statutory powers granted to the school corporation or which are necessary or desirable for the school corporation to conduct its affairs. However, certain powers may not be exercised by a school corporation unless a statute grants such a power to the school corporation. See IC 20-26-3-7.

B. School boards exercise plenary powers independent of other local government bodies.

HOME SCHOOLING: IC 20-8.1-3-17(h), IC 20-33-2-12, 20, 21 and 28, IC 21-3-1.6-1.2, and IC 31-6-11-3, See Chapter Eleven in the main text and Attendance in this Article II of the supplement

POINTS OF EMPHASIS:

A. Home schools must register with the Indiana Department of Education.

B. School boards should consider a policy for placement and awarding credits for students re-entering the public schools from a home school environment.

H

IMMUNITY FROM NEGLIGENT ACTIONS: See Chapter Two and Chapter Three in the main text

POINTS OF EMPHASIS:

A. School corporation employees are granted "conditional immunity" so long as they are conducting themselves appropriately as a reasonable and prudent person under the policies and procedures adopted by the local school board.

IMMUNIZATIONS: IC 20-33-2-28 and IC 20-34-3-5; See Chapter Eleven in the main text and Attendance in this Article II of the supplement

POINTS OF EMPHASIS:

A. Proof of immunizations is required of students upon enrolling in a school corporation under statutes and regulations of the state of Indiana and the local county board of health.

B. Students may not be refused enrollment because of lack of records, but a reasonable period of time may be given for submission of these records. If records are not received, school corporations may begin an exclusion process.

C. Students may be allowed not to have immunizations based on religious grounds.

INTERNET USAGE:

POINTS OF EMPHASIS:

A. School corporations and schools should develop internet usage policies and procedures.

B. Parents should be made aware of all internet usage policies.

C. It is suggested parents sign and return an acknowledgement of receipt of these policies.

D. Internet usage is protected by the First Amendment of the U.S. Constitution in connection with freedom of speech and press. Hazelwood School District v. Kuhlmeier, op. cit. is a fundamental case.

ALPHABETICAL QUICK REFERENCE FOR SCHOOL ADMINISTRATORS   135

LEGAL SETTLEMENT/RESIDENCE: IC 20-26-11; See Chapter One and Chapter Eleven in the main text

POINTS OF EMPHASIS:

A. If the student is under eighteen (18) years of age, or is over that age but is not emancipated, the legal settlement/residence of the student is in the attendance area of the school corporation where the student's parents reside.

B. In the case of a student whose mother and father are divorced the legal settlement/residence of the student is the school corporation whose attendance area contains the residence of the parent with whom the student is living in the following situations:

1. Where no court order has been made establishing the custody of the student; or

2. Where both parents have agreed on the parent or person with whom the student will live.

C. If the parents cannot support the student and the student is being supported by, cared for by, and living with, some other person the legal settlement/residence of the student is in the attendance area where the other person resides. The school corporation may, if the facts are in dispute, condition acceptance of the student's legal settlement on the appointment of that person as legal guardian or custodian of the student.

D. If the student is married and living with a spouse, the legal settlement/residence of that student is in the attendance area of the school corporation where the student and the student's spouse reside.

E. In the case of a student whose parents are living outside the United States, maintain no permanent home, and have placed the student in the home of another person, the legal settlement/residence of the student is in the attendance area where the other person resides.

F. If the student is emancipated, the legal settlement/residence is the attendance area of the school corporation of the student's residence.

G. If the legal settlement/residence of the student changes after the student has begun attending school in a school corporation in any given school year, the student may complete the current semester at that school corporation.

LICENSURE: IC 20-28-5, IC 28-4-1 et seq. and 515 IAC 1-1-1 et seq.; See Chapter Four in the main text

POINTS OF EMPHASIS:

A. The Division of Professional Standards of the Indiana Department of Education (DPS-IDOE) is responsible for the licensing of teachers, administrators, directors, and school services employees.

B. All applicants for a teacher's license must submit a limited criminal history.

C. The DPS-IDOE cannot issue a license unless the applicant has demonstrated proficiency on a written exam in the areas of basic reading, writing, mathematics, pedagogy, and knowledge of content area. If the applicant is seeking administrative or director licensure, leadership proficiency must be demonstrated on a written exam.

D. An applicant cannot get a license if the Indiana Department of Revenue indicates the applicant has a delinquent tax liability.

E. The DPS-IDOE must permanently revoke the license of a person who is known to have been convicted of a felony as listed under Indiana law.

ALPHABETICAL QUICK REFERENCE FOR SCHOOL ADMINISTRATORS   137

MEDICAL AND MEDICINES: IC 20-34-3-2 & 5, IC 25-22.5-1-2, IC 34-30-14-1 et. seq., 511 IAC 7-21-8 and 511 IAC 7-6-7(a); See Chapter Seven in the main text (In Loco Parentis)

POINTS OF EMPHASIS:

A. A child is exempt from medical testing, immunizations and treatment on religious grounds or provides a certificate of examination from an Indiana doctor.

B. A parent has the right to have his/her child examined by his/her physician rather than the school corporation's physician.

C. Parents have the right to receive a note from officials of the school corporation describing a child's illness or infestation when a child is sent home.

D. A parent has the right to receive medical care at a public facility when his/her child is sent home for illness or infestation and cannot afford private care.

E. A parent has the right to have a local health official decide when a child is seeking to be readmitted when school officials disagree with the parent's doctor.

F. Parents must consent in writing for the administration of medication at school.

G. School corporation staff should receive training, which should be recorded, in order to dispense any type of medication at school or on school field trips.

NEGLIGENCE: IC 34-13-3-4 and IC 34-13-4-1; See Chapter Two in the main text and Immunity from Negligent Actions in this Article II of the supplement

POINTS OF EMPHASIS:

A. Negligence is defined in the law as a standard of care a prudent person in the same situation would exercise.

B. An administrator of the school corporation is to provide a safe environment to protect children from harm.

C. Contributory negligence can be inferred if the person has contributed to the harm or alleged harm that has been suffered.

D. Indiana Tort Claims Act enacted by the General Assembly cap damage liability of a school corporation to $300,000 per incident ($5,000,000 with multiple plaintiffs).

E. A parent who is assisting the school corporation in an activity sponsored by the school corporation is limited to a maximum liability of $5,000 except in certain situations and the parent meets definition of a parent as described under Indiana law.

F. Common sense dictates that field trips will be safe with proper notification, qualified bu
    drivers and/or approved walking route, sufficient sponsors, and permission forms signed b
    legal guardians, however, a tort liability claim for negligence can still occur.

G. School corporations must carry sufficient liability insurance on their employees to cove
    them in the event of a lawsuit.

H. A comprehensive risk management program should be adopted by the school board to
    minimize negligence.

ALPHABETICAL QUICK REFERENCE FOR SCHOOL ADMINISTRATORS   139

PRAYER: See Chapter Three and Chapter Twelve in the main text

POINTS OF EMPHASIS:

A. Students may voluntarily pray in the school on their own time or free time so long as it does not pose a substantial disruption to the school environment. They may not infringe on others students' rights or force others to listen.

B. Religious organizations must be allowed to meet at school if other non-curricular clubs are allowed to meet.

C. No prohibition exists at the state or federal level for student-initiated religious speech or activities such as prayer, but the school may not advance or sponsor such speech or activities.

PROCEDURAL DUE PROCESS: IC 20-33-8; See Chapter Six in the main text and Discipline in this Article II of the supplement

POINTS OF EMPHASIS:

A. An administrator may take any action concerning the administrator's school or a school activity within the administrator's jurisdiction that is reasonably necessary to carry out or prevent interference with an educational function or the school purposes.

B. An administrator may assign up to 120 hours of community service for disciplinary reasons.

C. An administrator may suspend a student for not more than 10 school days for any single offense.

D. The administrator must conduct a meeting before suspension that

    1.   gives a written or oral statement of charges;

    2.   gives a summary of the evidence; and

    3.   gives a opportunity for student to explain his/her conduct.

E. Following the suspension, the administrator must send a written statement to the parent of the suspended student describing the conduct of the student and the action taken by the administrator.

F. When a student is expelled, the parent has a right to a hearing.

G. A hearing officer is appointed by the school board.

O-P

H. The hearing officer can be legal counsel or a member of the administrative staff of the school corporation so long as such person is not involved in the events leading to the expulsion.

I. The school board does not have to hear appeals.

J. If the parents appeal to the court system, the judicial review is limited to the issue of whether the school board acted without following the procedures required under law.

K. If a student is at least sixteen (16) years of age when expelled, the school corporation may require one or more of the following before allowing such a student to re-enroll:

1. an alternative school or alternative education program;

2. evening classes; or

3. classes established for students who are at least sixteen (16) years of age.

ALPHABETICAL QUICK REFERENCE FOR SCHOOL ADMINISTRATORS   141

SEARCH AND SEIZURE: IC 20-33-8; See Chapter Seven in the main text

POINTS OF EMPHASIS:

A. A school corporation must provide each student and each student's parent a copy of the rules of the governing body on searches of student lockers.

B. A student who uses a locker that is the property of the school corporation is presumed to have no expectation of privacy in that locker.

C. An administrator may search a student's locker at any time.

D. A school corporation and its employees must have only reasonable suspicion to search.

E. Law enforcement officers can assist school employees in searches if approved by the school board.

F. While strip searches are legal and have been upheld in courts of law, they are often found to be too intrusive and in violation of the Fourth Amendment of the U.S. Constitution. Given their intrusive nature, probable cause, not just reasonable suspicion, should be established as a basis for the search.

Q-S

TEACHER DISMISSAL: IC 20-28-7-1; See Chapter Four in the main text

POINTS OF EMPHASIS:

A. A permanent or semi-permanent teacher may be discharged for one or more of the following grounds:

1. Immorality;

2. Insubordination;

3. Neglect of duty;

4. Incompetence;

5. Justifiable decrease in the number of teaching positions;

6. A conviction of a felony; or

7. Other good and just cause.

B. When the cause of cancellation is based on 1, 2, or 6 above, the cancellation is effective immediately. When the cause of cancellation is based on 3, 4, 5, or 7 above, the cancellation is effective at the end of the school term following cancellation.

C. An indefinite contract may not be canceled for political or personal reasons.

D. Procedures for discharge of nonpermanent teacher.

1. The principal must provide the nonpermanent teacher's written evaluation by January 1. If the teacher submits a written request within thirty (30) days of receiving the evaluation, the principal must provide the teacher with an additional evaluation.

2. Before May 1, the school board must vote in a public meeting on the non-renewal of the contract.

3. On or before May 1, the school corporation must notify the teacher of the school board's decision to not renew the contract. The notice must be in writing and delivered in person or by registered or certified mail.

4. The teacher has fifteen (15) days from receipt of the notice of non-renewal to request a written statement of reasons for the non-renewal.

5. The written statement of reasons may be developed in executive session and it is not considered a public document.

6. The teacher may request a conference at any time and the conference must be held

ALPHABETICAL QUICK REFERENCE FOR SCHOOL ADMINISTRATORS   143

within ten (10) days of receipt of the request.

7. The teacher may have a representative at any conference.

8. If the conference is with the school board it will be in executive session unless the teacher requests a public conference.

9. The school board must affirm or reverse its position on non-renewal of the contract in a public meeting within ten (10) days after the conference with the teacher.

E. Procedures for discharge of semi-permanent or permanent teacher.

1. The superintendent must issue a notice containing the date, time, and place for consideration by the school board of cancellation of the teacher's contract. For a semi-permanent teacher, the date of consideration can be at any time. For a permanent teacher, however, the date of consideration must be no later than the last student day.

2. The notice must be personally delivered or mailed by certified mail, return receipt requested, at least thirty (30), but no more than forty (40), days before the date of consideration.

3. The teacher has fifteen (15) days from receipt of the notice of consideration to file a written request for a hearing before the school board. If the teacher fails to request a hearing within the required timeframe, the teacher has waived any right to a hearing.

4. The teacher may request, in writing, at any time, a written statement of reasons for the consideration. If requested, the written statement of reasons must be provided within five (5) days of receipt of the written request. The reasons must be specific enough for the teacher to understand the charges against him/her and to allow the preparation of a defense.

5. The superintendent must issue a notice containing the date, time, and place of the hearing before the school board. The teacher must be given at least five (5) days' notice of the hearing. The hearing may not be any earlier than five (5) days after the request is received.

6. If the reason for cancellation of the teacher's contract is performance-related, the hearing with the school board may be held in executive session. If, however, the reason for cancellation is a justifiable decrease in teaching positions (or reduction in force) and performance is not a criterion in the decision, the hearing before the school board must be in a public meeting.

7. At the hearing the teacher is entitled to a full statement of the reasons for the proposed cancellation. All statutory grounds that form the basis for the cancellation should be stated.

8. The teacher is also entitled to be heard, to present testimony of witnesses and other evidence relevant to the reasons for cancellation.

9. The superintendent must give a recommendation to the school board on the cancellation of the contract. This is a condition precedent to the cancellation. The superintendent must give the recommendation whether or not the teacher requested a hearing.

10. The school board must adopt written findings of fact and conclusions of law on which it based its decision.

11. The school board must vote in a public meeting on the cancellation. The school board's vote must be reflected in the school board's minutes of the meeting.

12. Notice of the school board's decision should be sent to the teacher, either in person or by certified mail. Notice should be given as soon as practical after the board's decision.

13. A semi-permanent or permanent teacher may be suspended from duty pending the cancellation proceedings. Any suspension must be *with pay*, including salary and fringe benefits.

TEACHER RECORDS: IC 5-14-3-1 et seq.; See Chapter Four in the main text

POINTS OF EMPHASIS:

A. "Public Record" means any writing, paper, report, study, map, photograph, book, card, tape recording, or other material that is created, received, retained, maintained, or filed by or with a public agency.

B. Any person may inspect and copy the public records of any public agency during the regular business hours of the agency, except for information declared:

1. confidential by state statute; or

2. personnel files of employees and files of applicants for public employment; except for name and compensation, information relating to the status of any formal charges, or the factual bases for a disciplinary action in which final action has been taken and resulted in the employee being suspended, demoted, or discharged.

C. A request for inspection or copying must:

1. identify with reasonable particularity the record being requested; and

2. be at the discretion of the school corporation in writing on or in a form provided by the school corporation.

ALPHABETICAL QUICK REFERENCE FOR SCHOOL ADMINISTRATORS   145

D. A school corporation may not disclose to commercial entities for commercial purposes:

   1.   a list of employees of a public agency;

   2.   a list of persons attending conferences or meetings at a state institution of higher education; or

   3.   a list of students who are enrolled in a public school.

TENURE: IC 20-28-6-8 et seq. and IC 20-28-10-2; See Chapter Four in the main text

POINTS OF EMPHASIS:

A. A teacher in a school corporation, who has served under contract for five (5) or more successive years and at any time enters into a teacher's contract for further service with that school corporation, becomes a permanent teacher of that school corporation.

B. When a contract between the school corporation and a permanent teacher expires by its terms, that contract is considered to continue indefinitely as an indefinite contract.

C. An indefinite contract remains in force until the permanent teacher reaches seventy-one (71) years of age unless it is:

   1.   replaced by a new contract signed by both parties; or

   2.   canceled through termination of the teacher.

D. Service under a temporary contract does not count toward achieving permanent status.

E. Service under a supplemental service teacher's contract counts toward tenure when a teacher serves more than one hundred twenty (120) days.

F. A leave of absence does not break the chain of successive years, but the time on leave does not count toward reaching permanent status.

G. Review the school board policy and the master contract for teacher tenure rights in assignment, reduction-in-force, and transfer of teachers.

TITLE IX: 20 U.S.C.A. § 1681; See Chapter Nine in the main text

POINTS OF EMPHASIS:

A. Enacted to protect rights of students and employees to prohibit discrimination based on gender in educational programs or activities in institutions receiving federal funds.

B. The Office of Civil Rights (OCR) of the U.S. Department of Education in the administrative agency is empowered to enforce Title IX.

C. The original Title IX was amended in 1988 to make it clear that discrimination was prohibited.

D. Violation of Title IX may result in the loss of federal funds to the entire school corporation.

E. School corporations are obligated to take reasonable steps to prevent sexual harassment.

TORT LIABILITY: IC 20-26-5-4(17), IC 34-13-3-3 et seq., IC 34-13-4-1 and IC 34-13-4-2; See Chapter Two in the main text and Immunity for Negligent Actions in this Article II of the supplement

POINTS OF EMPHASIS:

A. A school corporation may defend any member of the school board or any employee of the school corporation in any suit arising out of his/her duties for, or employment with, the school corporation, provided the school board determines by resolution that such action was taken in good faith. Tort liability might also involve parent helpers, substitute teachers and part-time employees, and any other individual recognized as having employeee or non-employee status with a school corporation.

B. A school corporation may purchase insurance to cover the liability of itself or its employees.

C. Plaintiffs seeking recovery against a school corporation and/or school employees must file a claim with the school corporation within one hundred eighty (180) days after the loss occurs.

D. Within ninety (90) days of the filing of a claim, the school corporation must notify the claimant in writing of its approval or denial of the claim.

E. School corporation personnel can be held individually liable for civil damage if their conduct violates clearly established statutory or constitutional rights of which a reasonable person would have known.

F. Schoool corporations should provide in-service training for staff regarding the staff's duty to provide proper student supervision on school grounds and fieldtrips. School corporations should emphasize that the standard of care is what a reason and prudent person would exercise in a similar situation or activity.

G. Before leaving on a fieldtrip make sure parental permission slips are signed and the slips contain specific information detailing foreseeable risks.

TRANSPORTATION: IC 20-27-5

POINTS OF EMPHASIS:

A. School board may, but is not required to, provide transportation. If a school board chooses to provide transportation, it must have the necessary equipment and drivers.

B. If a school board chooses to provide transportation, it also must provide transportation to parochial school students who live on the regular school routes.

C. The school board sets the number of chaperones on each bus during a school activity.

D. School bus drivers are subject to random drug testing processes and procedures as outlined by the school board.

E. Special purpose buses (as determined by the State School Bus Committee) may be used to provide transportation of school children from one school to another, but should not be used to transport school children between their residence and school.

VACCINATIONS: See Immunizations in this Article II of the supplement and Medical and Medicines in this Article II of the supplement

VOLUNTEERS: See Criminal Background Checks in this Article II of the supplement

POINTS OF EMPHASIS:

A. School corporations should adopt policies and/or administrative guidelines on the use of volunteers.

B. Volunteers should be defined and possibly required to complete criminal records checks.

C. Volunteers should probably receive training before being allowed to volunteer.

D. School corporations have the right to allow or deny the opportunity to volunteer.

ALPHABETICAL QUICK REFERENCE FOR SCHOOL ADMINISTRATORS   149

<u>WAIVER</u>: IC 20-18-2-17, IC 20-30-2-1 through 6,, 511 IAC 6.1-3-1, IC 31-32-5-1; See Chapter Six in the main text

POINTS OF EMPHASIS:

A. School funding of school corporations is based on at least 180 days of student instruction and at least 910 hours of instructional time. A waiver may be granted for a 2 hour late start time and 2 hour early dismissal due to an emergency such as weather or power failure. Beyond the 2 hours, only the State Superintendent of Public Instruction can wavie the minimum days and time requirements.

B. A child's rights are guaranteed under both United State and Indiana Constitution and may be waived only in specific circumstances.

C. Hearing rights under due process procedures can be waived by the parents of the child.

<u>WITHDRAWAL</u>: See Attendance

U-V

W-Z